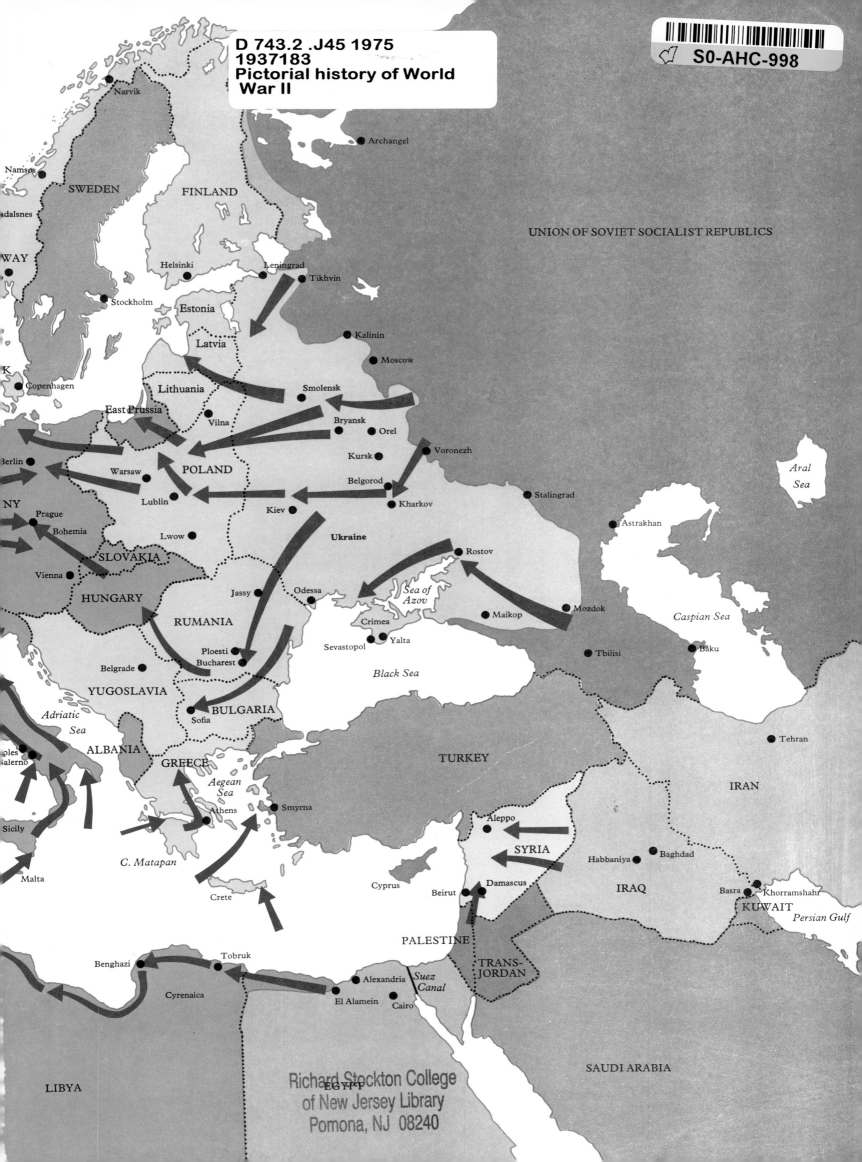

Narvik

Namsos

SWEDEN

FINLAND

adalsnes

WAY

Helsinki

Stockholm

Copenhagen

Leningrad

Archangel

UNION OF SOVIET SOCIALIST REPUBLICS

Estonia

Latvia

Tikhvin

Kalinin

Moscow

Lithuania

East Prussia

Smolensk

Vilna

Bryansk

Orel

Kursk

Voronezh

Aral
Sea

Berlin

Warsaw

POLAND

Belgorod

Stalingrad

Astrakhan

NY

Prague

Lublin

Kiev

Kharkov

Bohemia

Lwow

Ukraine

SLOVAKIA

Vienna

Rostov

Maikop

Mozdok

Caspian Sea

HUNGARY

Jassy

Odessa

Sea of
Azov

RUMANIA

Crimea

Sevastopol

Yalta

Tbilisi

Baku

Ploesti

Bucharest

Black Sea

Belgrade

YUGOSLAVIA

BULGARIA

Sofia

Adriatic
Sea

ALBANIA

GREECE

Aegean
Sea

TURKEY

Tehran

IRAN

ples
alerno

Athens

Smyrna

Aleppo

Sicily

C. Matapan

SYRIA

Habbaniya

Baghdad

Malta

Crete

Cyprus

Beirut

Damascus

IRAQ

Basra

Khorramshahr

KUWAIT

Persian Gulf

PALESTINE

TRANS-
JORDAN

Benghazi

Tobruk

Alexandria

Suez
Canal

Cyrenaica

El Alamein

Cairo

SAUDI ARABIA

LIBYA

EGYPT

PICTORIAL WORLD

HISTORY OF
WAR II

PATRICK JENNINGS

LONGMEADOW
PRESS

First published in the USA in 1975 by
Longmeadow Press, PO Box 16, Rowayton Station
Norwalk, Connecticut 06853

© 1975 Hennerwood Publications Limited

ISBN 0 904230 10 4

Produced by Mandarin Publishers Limited
Hong Kong

Printed in Hong Kong

Jacket: front, U.S. Marine Corps; back,
Robert Hunt Library; flaps, Imperial
War Museum.

CONTENTS

BLITZKRIEG -POLAND

The attack on Poland was an attempt by Hitler to seize yet another country in Europe with hardly a shot being fired. But the attack started the Second World War.

Above: *Hitler and Paul Joseph Goebbels, his propaganda minister (right), attend a demonstration in honour of President von Hindenburg in the early days of the rule of the Third Reich in Germany.*

Above: *Prime Minister Neville Chamberlain signs the Munich Agreement of 30 September, 1938, which sealed the fate of Czechoslovakia.*

World War Two began at 0445 on the morning of 1 September, 1939. For several years British and French diplomats had tried to bargain with Hitler, but their attempts to appease his appetite for power and territory had utterly failed. He had bluffed them in March 1936 when he remilitarized the Rhineland. Exactly two years later he annexed Austria, while Britain and France still did nothing. Later in 1938 he staked his claim to the German-speaking Sudetenland area of Czechoslovakia, comprising most of that country's defences and much of her industry. When Hitler threatened war if the annexation were not allowed to go ahead Britain and France acquiesced, signing the Munich agreement on 30 September. So far Hitler had only demanded territory inhabited by Germans. But when the Czechoslovak government collapsed in March 1939, Hitler in effect annexed most of the country, marching his troops into Prague (15 March) and declaring a protectorate over the rump state of Slovakia. Now, at last, the Western allies adopted a more resolute stance. On 31 March Britain made a defence pact with Poland, pledging intervention of her armed forces in the event of a German invasion. Britain was incapable of giving Poland aid, since Britain and France were tragically unready for war. Although arms production was already well under way, neither the British nor the French people were psychologically prepared to defend their European and worldwide interests. Nor were the respective governments prepared to settle their ideological differences with the Soviet Union, their obvious ally in any war against Germany.

When Hitler annexed Memel, a German-speaking enclave in Lithuania, (22 March), Italy, not to be outdone, overran Albania, (9 May). Two weeks later the two nations signed the Pact of Steel in Berlin. But in order to invade Poland, Hitler had to be sure that he would not be opposed by the Soviet Union. Stalin, who had just completed his purge of Russia's top-ranking military

Above: *Chamberlain returns in triumph from Munich to Hendon airfield near London, where he declared that the agreement he had reached with Hitler, Mussolini and Daladier meant 'peace for our time'. World War II was less than a year away.*
Below: *Hitler on the road from Prague to Brünn after his take-over of Czechoslovakia, 15 March 1939.* Left: *Adolf Hitler, Führer of the Third Reich. His National Socialist movement had gained few supporters until the Great Depression in 1929. By August 1934 he had gained complete political control under the new title of 'leader' Führer.*

German advance 1-14 Sept 1939

Polish counterattack and retreat 9 Sept

Red Army invades from the East 17 Sept

Polish Poznan Army surrendered 19 Sept

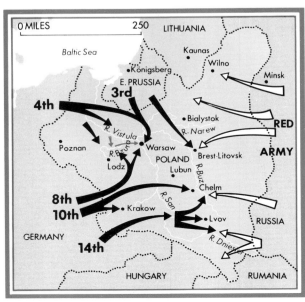

Above: *The Molotov–Ribbentrop Pact secured Hitler's eastern flank and effectively partitioned Poland between Germany and the Soviet Union. The happy conspirators who shocked the world celebrate their unholy alliance. Left to right: Ribbentrop, German Foreign Minister, Gaus, Under Secretary of State, Joseph Stalin, and Russian Foreign Minister Molotov. Above right: Polish cavalry advance toward the front. They were among the last cavalry units to be used in modern warfare. Below: Stukas of the Luftwaffe made short work of Polish cities as the high-pitched shriek of their dive-bombers struck terror into the hearts of the civilian population. Bottom: These brave but foolish Polish cavalrymen had no chance against the Pzkw-1 tanks of the Wehrmacht.*

staff, and whose armies were not yet prepared to fight against Germany, decided that if he could not reach a bargain with the Western allies, he would come to an agreement with his arch-enemy, Nazi Germany. When, on 23 August, 1939, the world woke up to the stunning news that Hitler and Stalin had signed a non-aggression pact, it became clear that unless Britain were to revoke her pledge to protect Poland, war was inevitable. In a secret clause to their treaty, Germany and Russia agreed to partition Poland, the Russian share being the territory in the east (over one-third of the country's area) which the Poles had snatched from her after World War One, as well as most of the Baltic states. Now the way was clear for Hitler to take not only the German-speaking territory of Danzig hitherto under the protection of the League of Nations, but the whole of Poland up to the Curzon Line. When the dawn attack occurred on 1 September, the question was not whether Germany had the power to win; it was whether Britain and France would do anything concrete to prevent the inevitable German victory.

Britain and France did declare war, (3 September) but virtually refused to wage it. On the common border with France, only 33 German divisions were placed along the still uncompleted West Wall, of which at least 25 were second-rate. France, although possessing command of the air and over 70 divisions, did nothing, enabling Hitler to concentrate all his might on the Polish invasion. While the RAF dropped leaflets over Germany, the Nazis launched a new style of warfare – blitzkrieg, or 'lightning war'. Stuka dive bombers strafed Polish airfields, wiping out most of her puny obsolete air force on the ground within the first 48 hours. Meanwhile, from Pomerania, Silesia, East Prussia and Slovakia the Panzer divisions thrust into Poland, fanning out in three directions. Polish armed forces, unwisely placed along the German frontier, slow to mobilize and hopelessly outnumbered, were quickly surrounded and overwhelmed. Their horse cavalry (the sole area in which the Poles were numerically superior) vainly attacked columns of German tanks. The only effective opposition took place during a counter-attack across the

Above: *The Ju-87 Stuka in action over Poland. These dive-bombers descended rapidly, coming in low for precision destruction of enemy targets. Their equally rapid ascent made them almost impervious to the poorly organized anti-aircraft fire of the Poles, although they were highly vulnerable to crossfire from enemy planes. The Polish air force was virtually wiped out, however, within the first 48 hours.*

Poland is divided according to a secret pact between Germany and Russia:

To Germany

To Russia

Reindeer assist the ski-borne troops of the Finnish Army in the Winter War against Russia 1939–40.

Above: Finnish machine-gunners in winter gear defend their position against the advancing Russians. The heroic stand of Finland convinced both Hitler and the Western Powers that the Soviet Army could not withstand an assault by the Wehrmacht. These illusions were shattered in 1941 when the Germans were halted before the gates of Moscow and Leningrad. Below and right: A church in Helsinki is set ablaze after a Soviet air raid during the Winter War.

River Bzura on the night of 9–10 September, but this was quickly repulsed. Within just over a week Warsaw was surrounded and most of Poland was already in German hands. Even Russia, who anticipated the attack and was fully expecting to profit from it, was astonished at the speed of the victory. On 17 September Soviet troops, at a cost of less than a thousand lives, moved into the remainder of what had been the Polish state, as German Stukas hammered away at the beleaguered Polish capital, rapidly reducing it to rubble. The era of total war had begun, and Warsaw was the first to feel its sting. The city held out valiantly until the 27th. Shortly before the capitulation a high-ranking German intelligence officer remarked that Warsaw was a 'dead city'. Russia annexed the eastern half of Poland, which was predominantly non-Polish anyway, and the rest of the country came under the 'protection' of the Third Reich.

The fall of Poland brought dramatic consequences in Eastern Europe. On 30 November Stalin attacked Finland, aiming to secure his northern flank in case Hitler tried to double-cross him by attempting an invasion of the Soviet Union through that country. Field Marshal Mannerheim's gallant soldiers were better equipped for winter warfare than the Russians, despite the insurmountable odds facing them, and held them for three months, until Finland finally capitulated on 12 March, 1940, and the Russo–Finnish frontier was pushed back both near Leningrad and in the north. Soon afterwards Russia moved into Estonia, Latvia and most of Lithuania, and annexed them.

The lessons of the Polish campaign and the Russo–Finnish war were not lost on London and Paris, as the Allies steeled themselves to defend Scandinavia if Hitler turned west. The blitzkrieg of September 1939 was followed by the 'sitzkrieg' of 1939–40. Britain and France waged only a war of words against the Third Reich, while preparing to meet the storm soon to blow in their direction.

Germans offload equipment into a Norwegian port. Their forces took most of the main coastal cities with ease, but their attempt to seal off Narvik encountered heavy British resistance for almost two months until they forced an evacuation. The Norwegians never accepted Nazi rule and Germany was obliged to send tens of thousands of troops to Scandinavia to maintain their occupation of these areas throughout the rest of the war.

BLITZKRIEG -SCANDINAVIA

Hitler's strike to the North altered Allied public opinion in a way that the attack in Eastern Europe could never have done. The invasion of Norway and Denmark swept away most of the support for appeasement in Britain and France.

The phoney war of 1939–40 seems today like a never-never land of vague, impossible hopes and unrealistic dreams. The French, although open to aerial bombardment, felt safe behind their Maginot Line – a network of huge concrete blockhouses along the German border with guns which pointed in only one direction. Britain hesitated to bomb Germany for fear of retaliation on herself and France, and more than one Conservative MP expressed shock at the suggestion that bombs should replace leaflets when the RAF flew over the Rhine. Meanwhile, when it became clear that the Allies would not make peace with Germany after the fall of Poland, Hitler planned his next move – to the north. The Führer, expecting a British landing in Norway, decided to strike first. Seizure of the Norwegian ports would effectively prevent Britain using them to blockade German harbours. These ports were used for the export of Swedish iron ore, vital to the German war machine. The Chamberlain government in London was reluctant to provoke German wrath, but Winston Churchill, First Lord of the Admiralty, was not. Although the Cabinet rejected his plan to land troops in Norway during March 1940 (thereby breaching Norwegian neutrality) he decided to make preparations for a landing the moment Germany invaded Scandinavia or seemed on the brink of doing so.

Hitler intended to attack Norway and Denmark in early spring. The OKW *(Oberkommando der Wehrmacht)* was placed in charge of the operation, and little resistance from either country was expected. The problem was how far Britain would go in order to protect the Norwegian ports and airfields. The plan, therefore, was to attack all the major ports from Oslo to Narvik in one bold stroke, with simultaneous parachute drops on Norway's major airfields. Vidkun Quisling had already been earmarked as the new Norwegian leader.

The invasion, set for 9 April, looked risky for two reasons. First, the British took the initiative on 8 April by laying minefields in Norwegian waters. Second, heavy storms at sea threatened to ruin the entire plan. German staff work, however, proved to be impeccable. Coal ships containing invasion troops were already lying at anchor in some Norwegian harbours before the 9th. On that day Norway was hit by gales and snowstorms. The full fury of the Wehrmacht and the Luftwaffe struck as well. At the same time the

Germans attacked Denmark. King Christian X, unwilling to sacrifice the lives of over 14,000 soldiers, capitulated almost at once. King Haakon II of Norway, however, was prepared to risk his army of 13,000 and his own life. He refused to surrender and escaped to a remote country village, hoping for Allied assistance. Despite the warnings of the attack, the Germans met little effective resistance on the first day, when most of the major ports, including Oslo, Stavanger, Bergen, Trondheim and Narvik, were captured. Even though some, like Bergen, were taken within hours, the path to victory did not run quite as straight as the Wehrmacht would have wished. On the previous day, near Lillesund, the Polish submarine *Orzel* had sunk the German transport *Rio de Janeiro* on its way to 'protect' Bergen. There were several actions by British ships, but no general engagement with the Germans took place. The Norwegians, however, did rather better against enormous odds. On the day of the invasion the German cruiser *Blücher* was set on fire and sunk at Oscarsborg, hit by guns, which predated the Boer War, from a fortress built during the Crimean War. The pocket battleship *Lützow* too, was badly damaged.

Yet Norway, for all her determination, had little chance against Nazi Germany unless she received considerable help from Britain and France and this was not forthcoming. The French role was ludicrous. The few men who were landed had neither snowshoes nor skis; and there were no supporting tanks or guns. What is more, the ship

Top left: *German soldiers guard the North Cape, the rim of northern Europe. By June 1940 Nazi troops controlled Europe from the Arctic Circle to the Pyrenees.* Above left: *A desolate anchorage in northern Norway, patrolled by German coastal batteries and soldiers after their occupation of the Norwegian coast.*

Above right: *The burning harbour of Narvik, with transports sunk by British destroyers in the first battle of Narvik, and two German destroyers alongside the quay in the foreground.* Below: *After the occupation of Norway the Germans were constantly on the alert for British raiders along the coast. German garrison troops take up their positions in one of these manoeuvres.*

carrying them was too big to enter Namsos harbour. British assistance was slow to arrive and at best half-hearted. Some troops were landed but far too late to make much difference – face-saving devices rather than effective counter-attacks. Three of the four main landings – at Andalsnes, Namsos and Bodo – failed and the Germans consolidated the gains they had made on the first day of the blitzkrieg, forcing British withdrawals from central Norway around the end of April. Only at Narvik (the vital iron-ore port) did the British meet with any degree of success. The town was taken on 28 May but evacuated on 8 June. It was the only clear-cut Allied victory of the war thus far. But Norway was already lost and Allied attention was by now diverted – rightly so – to the Low Countries and France.

Although the capitulation of Norway assured the Germans a regular supply of iron ore, many ports and airfields from which to operate against Britain, and another easy victory, the conquest of Scandinavia (for Sweden, though unoccupied and still neutral, was effectively in Hitler's pocket) proved a long-term drain on German resources. Further Allied attempts to reoccupy Norway could never be ruled out, and the Norwegian people put up fierce resistance throughout the war. Eventually the occupation of Norway and Denmark tied down 300,000 German troops who could have been put to use elsewhere.

In Britain the debate in the House of Commons after the Norwegian debacle was particularly fierce. General Auchinleck reported that the morale of the British troops in Norway was very low indeed: so was the morale of the Conservative Party, which abandoned Neville Chamberlain and his feeble leadership. There was a growing demand in the country for an all-party government to carry on with the war, and Labour simply would not serve under the 'man of Munich'. Chamberlain soon realized, after the heated debate in the House on 7–8 May, that he could no longer command the leadership of his party or of the country, and on 9 May he conferred with the only two men who could lead a united nation against the enemy: Lord Halifax and Winston Churchill. Chamberlain's choice was Halifax, whose continuing appeasement-oriented views mirrored his own. But it was Churchill who triumphed and went to Buckingham Palace to kiss hands on 10 May. On the same day that Britain found its leader at last, Germany struck at the Low Countries and France. The phoney war was over. The War in the West, and the fight for Britain's survival, had begun.

Left: *A column of smoke rises above the wreck of the German cruiser* Königsberg, *sunk by British Skua dive bombers at Bergen. This was the first warship to be sunk by dive bombing. German warship losses were so heavy that there were not enough to launch against Britain in the summer of 1940.* Top right: *German seaplanes in a Norwegian fjord help guard the coast against a British attack.* Centre right: *The Wehrmacht forces its way into a burning Norwegian village during the first days of the Blitzkrieg in Scandinavia.* Right: *Infantry clearing a road.*

German invasion of Denmark and Norway, started 9 April 1940

14.5.40

German advance and dates of capture

15.4.40
8.6.40

Allied landings, (top date) and later withdrawals, (bottom date)

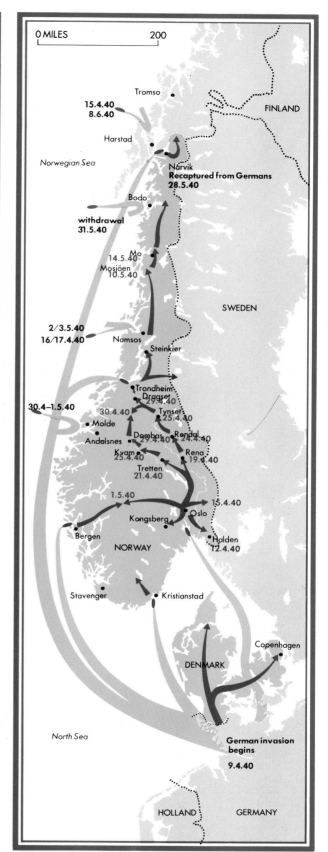

0 MILES — 200

Tromso

15.4.40
8.6.40

FINLAND

Harstad

Narvik
Recaptured from Germans
28.5.40

Norwegian Sea

Bodo

withdrawal
31.5.40

Mo
14.5.40
Mosjöen
10.5.40

SWEDEN

2/3.5.40
16/17.4.40

Namsos

Steinkier

Trondheim
29.4.40
Dragset

30.4–1.5.40

30.4.40
Tynset
25.4.40

Molde

Dombas
29.4.40
Andalsnes
Kvam
25.4.40
Tretten
21.4.40

Rendal.
24.4.40
Rena
19.4.40

1.5.40

Kongsberg

Oslo

15.4.40

Bergen

NORWAY

Halden
12.4.40

Stavenger

Kristianstad

North Sea

Copenhagen

DENMARK

German invasion
begins

9.4.40

HOLLAND   GERMANY

BLITZKRIEG -THE WEST

Before Germany completed her conquest of Norway, her attack in the West had begun. Hitler expected France to put up a stiff resistance, and he hoped to overwhelm the Low Countries before effective British and French aid could reach them. In the early hours of 10 May 1940 parachutists and heavy bombers of the Luftwaffe descended on Holland and Belgium.

Well before the fall of Norway, Hitler was making preparations for his most audacious attack thus far: the simultaneous invasion of Holland, Belgium, Luxembourg and France. Facing him was the seemingly impregnable Maginot Line and a French tank force which, even without the addition of British tanks on the Continent, outnumbered Germany's. His gamble was based, however, on the immoveable French apathy and disinclination for war as well as the obvious absence of coordination among the Allies; and he was proved right. In fact the greatest weaknesses of the Allied position lay in French leadership which was mediocre – particularly in the case of General Maurice Gamelin – and their lack of a strategic reserve, which would enable the Germans, should a breakthrough be accomplished, to operate at will behind French lines. It was as if a blank cheque was drawn in Hitler's name on the Bank of France. He was now prepared to cash it. The date – 10 May, 1940.

Despite repeated warnings from various intelligence sources that an attack was imminent, the

Above: *A German soldier keeps watch in a bombarded town in northern France. The sweep to the Channel took both the Allies and the Nazis by surprise.*

Below: *One of the British ships that didn't get away at Dunkirk. A combination of bad flying weather for the Luftwaffe and allied courage and good luck saved the evacuees who crossed the Channel, but thousands did not escape.*

Above: *The burning city of Rotterdam, whose centre was destroyed needlessly by German bombs on 14 May 1940, just as the Dutch were capitulating.*

Above: *The ruins of Rotterdam after its destruction. German hopes of winning Dutch public opinion over to acceptance of their New Order were ruined as well.* Below: *General Erwin Rommel and his staff check battle plans and maps of northern France.*

Top: *Infantrymen of the Wehrmacht during the sweep across northern France.* Above: *German soldiers in a Flemish town. The Belgians capitulated before the Dunkirk evacuation.* Below: *A German tank sweeps across northern France.*

Dutch were caught unprepared when German paratroops descended like winter snow from the the dawn skies. The excuse given was that the British were preparing to land in the Low Countries, thus violating Dutch and Belgian neutrality. In fact this was not far from being the case, but the Germans pressed ahead without waiting for a reply from the Dutch to their ultimatum to surrender at once. The Dutch government prepared to flee to England as their lines of defence crumbled in the face of Army Group B under General Fedor von Bock. Flooding the dikes failed to stop the German advance. While a ceasefire in Holland was being arranged on 14 May, a flight of Luftwaffe planes disobeyed instructions and bombed the centre of Rotterdam when the Dutch were on the point of capitulating. The heart of the greatest port in Europe was needlessly wiped out. It was an attack the Germans were soon to regret. The success of their wisely thought-out occupation policy depended upon correct behaviour toward the civilian population. This was observed – but to no avail. Most of the Dutch people resented the German occupation after the destruction of Rotterdam.

Meanwhile, as Allied troops surged forward into Belgium with eerie effortlessness, Army Group A under General Gerd von Rundstedt launched an attack with gliders and paratroopers on the powerful Belgian fort of Eben Emael near Liège, capturing it in 36 hours. This opening on the Belgian front left Brussels and Antwerp exposed. The Anglo–French counter-thrust was intended to create a solid front between Belgium and the Alps. In the meantime, however, General Erwin Rommel's tanks were penetrating the supposedly impassable forest of the Ardennes, and by 12 May German troops were on French soil near Sedan, scene of the French disaster of 1870. The next day they were across the Meuse and heading for unprotected open country – behind the Anglo–French lines. The Allies were caught in a trap of their own creation. Without any *masse de manoeuvre* (strategic reserve), all France south of this new German thrust was virtually undefended and as the Germans widened their sweep across the rolling hills of northern France, most of the British and French forces were pinned between two armies – the Panzers of Generals Paul von Kleist and Rommel advancing in the south and Army Group A moving through northern Flanders. Gamelin's deputy, General Georges, had a nervous breakdown, another French general committed suicide,

CHAMBRE DES DEPUTES

DEUTSCHLAND SIEGT AN ALLEN FRONTE[N]

Left: *A 'V' for
victory symbol over the
Chamber of Deputies in
Paris meant one thing
to the Nazis in France
and quite another to
the Resistance. The
motto 'Germany is
winning on all fronts'
hangs where parliamen-
tarians refused to vote
for defence expenditure
in the late 1930s.* Below
left: *British troops
surrender at Calais.*

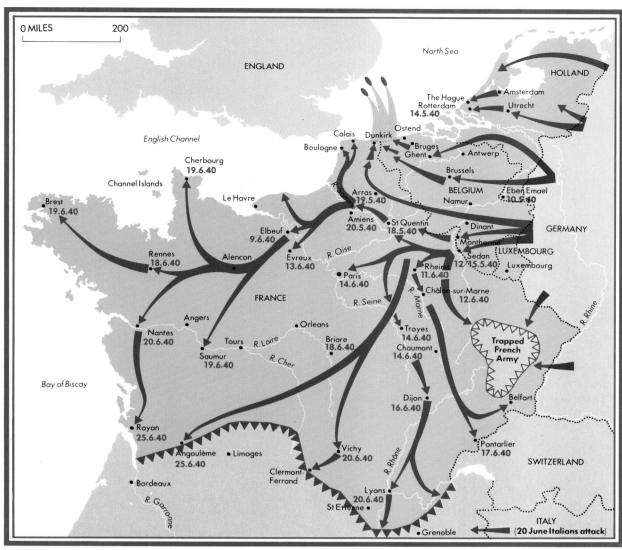

and Gamelin himself, who had sent some of his men on leave three days before the initial attack of 10 May, was sacked and replaced by General Maxime Weygand flown in especially from Syria. Weygand was 72. Marshal Philippe Pétain, the hero of Verdun, was appointed Deputy Premier; he was 85. By the time the Germans reached Amiens on 20 May, it was far too late for these ancient warhorses, or for Lord Gort, Commander of the British Expeditionary Force, to undo the damage already done. A reserve could not be created from thin air. General Heinz Guderian's tanks pressed forward to the Channel; the 2nd Panzer Division was the first to arrive there on the 20th. In the air the Germans were in command. The RAF had lost over half its bombers within three days of the opening of the blitz-krieg. The German breakthrough was complete and the trap was rapidly closing. The Battle of France was already lost.

Lord Gort was forced to issue the order to evacuate as soon as possible. Time was short, for if the Germans should cross France – a distance of 300 miles – in three days, how long would it take for them to travel some 30 miles up the coast to engage the British and French, who, with their Belgian colleagues, watched as the inexorable trap closed around them on three sides. Then Hitler ordered a halt. German tank commanders and crews were exhausted and needed a respite. But the British needed one even more. Evacu-ations began on 26 May, and by 29/30 May more

than 50,000 men were escaping daily. Goering had insisted that the mopping-up operation be left to the Luftwaffe, which, apart from ham-mering Rotterdam, had played only a minor role in the Battle of France thus far. By now a steady consumer of drugs, he hesitated, giving the British further breathing space. Rain and fog on 29 and 30 May gave the Allies another break from Luftwaffe attacks. When the weather broke on 1 June the men on the beaches of Dunkirk were distraught – exhausted and frustrated by the failure of the RAF to provide sufficient air cover; but Churchill was wisely saving them for the protection of Britain herself. Significantly, how-ever, in the clashes which did take place the RAF, operating from home airfields, did take a heavy toll of enemy aircraft, which were based on the Rhine. It was a portent which few recognized at the time.

Some 338,000 men were evacuated from Dun-kirk before the net closed; only 40,000 prisoners were taken. In France a further 190,000 were evacuated from ports in Normandy and from Bordeaux. Over 558,000 troops, a third of them non-British, were eventually transported to Britain from the Continent. Regarded as a triumph for the British Navy and a tribute to British perseverance in horrific conditions, the evacuation was actually a legacy of a staggering and overwhelming Allied defeat in France and the failure of the Luftwaffe and the Wehrmacht to close the Belgian pocket more quickly.

23

Dunkirk also gave the French forces south of the German lines some temporary relief. The remains of the French Army, however, were in no position to offer more than token resistance to the Wehrmacht. General Weygand tried to form a line of defence along the Aisne and the Somme, similar to that of World War One, but it soon crumbled. Germans crossed the Seine on 10 June, the day on which Mussolini, who had stood aloof from war until this moment, decided to risk an invasion of France. As Roosevelt so aptly put it, 'The hand that held the dagger struck it in the back of its neighbour.' The thrust was ineffectual. The Italians met some resistance, and got bogged down east of the Rhône. On 12 June Paris was declared an open city and victorious German soldiers paraded down the Champs Elysées two days later. The French government moved first to Tours, then to Bordeaux. Premier Paul Reynaud, who had begged pitifully and vainly for 'waves of planes' to hurl back the invader, resigned in favour of Marshal Pétain, who asked for an immediate armistice. The demand for a separate peace, despite treaty arrangements with Britain and Churchill's extraordinary last-minute offer of a union between the two countries, reflected the feeling in France that Britain had let them down. Air Marshal Sir Hugh Dowding had refused to sacrifice planes in France which would soon be needed to defend Britain – a wise decision, but one which the French could hardly be expected to understand.

On 22 June, in the same railway car at Compiègne where the armistice with a defeated Germany had been signed in 1918, France agreed to an unconditional surrender. The country was to be occupied, except for about one-third of territory in the south which would be ruled by Pétain from Vichy – a spa whose waters contained an aroma not dissimilar to that which shortly thereafter emanated from the government established there. French forces were to be disarmed and demobilized. Most French prisoners were retained until the end of the war. In a peace settlement with Italy, signed two days later, Mussolini received a reward for his miserable efforts: Nice and part of Savoy. Although General Charles de Gaulle, whose tank forces had fought as well as they could in the circumstances, created a Free French government in London, the Battle of France was over. The Battle of Britain was about to begin.

Right and far right: *The victory parade forms up to march down the Champs Elysees. Few Frenchmen turned out to watch the celebration, the most stunning humiliation of French arms in history. It dwarfed the fall of France in 1814 to Alexander I of Russia and the triumph of Prussia and von Moltke in 1870.*

Above: *The cover of the German wartime propaganda magazine* Signal *shows Dornier bombers over the Eiffel Tower, the symbol of the magnitude of the Nazi triumph. The leading article featured the capitulation of Paris, which was declared an open city as the Wehrmacht approached.* Above right: *This fortress of the Maginot Line was taken from the rear with ease. The heavy guns of the string of bunkers along the length of the Franco–German frontier could not swivel around and were useless once the Nazis had seized the rest of northern France. The defenders above were quickly overwhelmed, and the men below were trapped in the complex, pre-war labyrinths.*

Above: *Soldiers of the Wehrmacht, exhausted by the speed of their victory, doze in a Parisian street as the Nazis occupied the capital on 14 June 1940.*

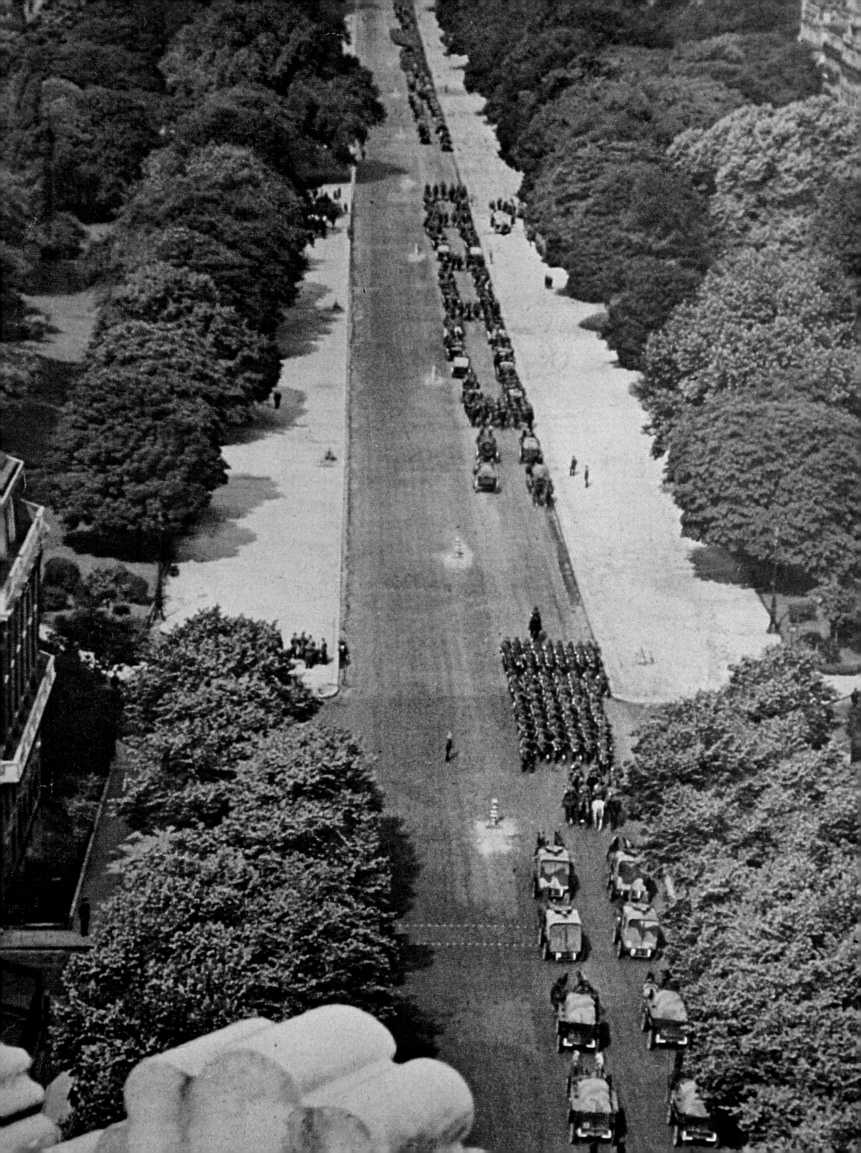

THE BATTLE OF BRITAIN

As the boats from Dunkirk reeled back to Britain Churchill and the War Cabinet started preparations for the expected German invasion. The Battle for Britain's survival was to start in the air five weeks after the evacuation.

In the summer of 1940 Britain stood alone. Winston Churchill announced in the House of Commons on 18 June: 'Let us therefore brace ourselves to our duties, and so bear ourselves that, if the British Empire and its Commonwealths last for a thousand years, men will still say: "This was their finest hour." ' But the situation looked desperate. The one power capable of helping Britain – the United States – was in the throes of an election campaign, in which the two main issues were Roosevelt's unprecedented attempt for a third term in the Presidency and the debate between the Republicans and Democrats in which each explained to the voters their reasons for not wanting America to enter the war. Churchill counted on America's entry into the war. He continued to count on it. Since before the turn of the century, Britain's industrial strength had been declining in comparison with that of the other industrial powers. By 1940 it was clear that without the help of at least one major industrial nation Britain could not liberate Europe on her own. Her position in the Far East and India was extremely precarious. Her lifeline of empire through the Mediterranean and Suez was threatened by Italy. She faced all of these problems, and the seemingly imminent invasion of her islands by Germany, quite alone. America could not help – yet.

Twenty divisions were earmarked by Hitler for Operation Sea Lion – the invasion of England. Whether or not he could have mounted a successful amphibious operation, even if Germany had won command of the skies over England and the Channel, is an open question. Certainly she did not win, nor could she ever have gained sufficient naval supremacy in the Channel for such a massive undertaking; and even if temporary naval superiority could have been won, the German flotilla in the summer of 1940 was too small to bring over men and equipment in sufficient strength unless

Right: Prime Minister Winston Churchill surveys defences on the British coast. In the anxious days of the summer of 1940 an invasion was expected nightly.

Above: *A squadron of Luftwaffe Me-109s*. Above left: *The Bank of England and the Royal Exchange after an air raid*. Left: *The Spitfire, symbol of the Battle of Britain*.

Below: Underground stations in London were turned into air raid shelters where people worked, dozed and chatted through the night. Below centre: Hermann Goering, the World War I air ace in charge of the Luftwaffe, who directed the attack against British airfields and cities. Right: Holborn Circus, London, ablaze during a night raid. Far right: German pilots struggle to stay afloat in a dinghy after bailing out over the Channel.

total mastery of the air were achieved. So everything hinged on one factor – command of the air. If the Luftwaffe were able to drive the RAF from the skies, German air attacks on British ships could render them ineffective. Then an amphibious landing could be mounted at leisure as and when sufficient German ships became available.

Although morale was high in the British Army, there were not enough men to guard the long British coasts against German landings at various points. Hitler's aim was to land 260,000 men on English shores within three days. If he could have achieved this, Britain would have lost her freedom. Had General Erhard Milch been given his way, the German plan might have succeeded. He wanted to follow the Dunkirk disaster by an immediate cross-Channel assault. But Hitler hesitated, still hoping for a negotiated peace with the United Kingdom, which he had always admired. He completely underestimated the strength of British resolve to fight to the end. This was no longer Neville Chamberlain's appeasement Britain. It was the Britain of Churchill, who promised to 'defend our island, what-

ever the cost may be.' America, given the political exigencies of the moment, sent what she could: 130 million rounds of ammunition, a half-million rifles, 100 million shells. But it was the air force that mattered. The Germans had over 2,800 planes at their disposal, over half of which were fighters – Me 109s and Me 110s. Against these the RAF had about 1,200 planes of the first rank, of which 800 were Spitfires or Hurricane fighters; 660 of them were operational on the eve of the Battle of Britain. But production of Spitfires had been stepped up by 500 per month. So if the RAF could hold its own for a while, all would be well.

But was there time? In the five weeks which elapsed between Dunkirk and the start of the Battle of Britain hundreds of British fighters had been built to replace the losses in France. The shortage of trained British pilots was another problem. This was partly solved by the circumstances of the battle itself, since British pilots who were shot down had a good chance to bail out and live to fight another day. This was an advantage denied to the protégés of the Luftwaffe masterminds, Ernst Udet and Hermann Goering.

Above: *Stirling bombers of the RAF made the first raids on Berlin, causing Hitler and Goering to take reprisals against London. This gave British air bases a much-needed breathing space. Left: Me-109s dominated the skies in the early stages of the Battle of Britain. If they had continued to attack British air fields rather than striking against cities, they could have cleared the skies of Spitfires and Hurricanes in preparation for an invasion.*

Above: *Spitfires strike back against the Me-109s. By October German plans to invade Britain were postponed indefinitely.*

German airmen shot down over Britain could hardly evade capture; and parachuting out in the Channel was tantamount to suicide. The British had two further advantages. The range of the German bombers – He 111s, Do 17s and Ju 88s – was such that with a full load they could not stay over Britain for more than a few minutes if they hoped to return safely. The fighters which accompanied them had an equally limited range. This was no problem for Spitfires and Hurricanes. They did not have to fly so far. Britain's second advantage lay in her now perfected radar system. A chain of 51 radar stations was in position along the coasts at the start of the war, and these were bolstered by a second line of radar stations hastily constructed after war had begun. These stations could signal the RAF well enough in advance to indicate the whereabouts of enemy planes before they reached the coastline, so that the Luftwaffe could be intercepted before too much damage was caused.

The Battle of Britain opened on 10 July when German bombers began attacking convoys in the Channel. But even now there was further breathing space, for it was not until the second week of August that German air strikes were intensified and that airfields in Britain were hit for the first time. Sir Hugh Dowding of Fighter Command estimated that German losses would have to be four times as heavy as those of the British in the early stages for the RAF to have a fighting chance. This was almost accomplished in August and September. Goering increased the proportion of

fighters to bombers to protect his more vulnerable aircaft. The Me 109, though an excellent plane, was not best equipped for escort missions, and divebombing Stukas in the context of this battle were useless. The Luftwaffe would have to destroy the RAF in the air, and wipe out their bases on the ground. Since each bomber required two fighters for protection, the numbers of Me 109s and 110s available to fight the Spitfires and Hurricanes were thereby reduced. Reinforcements from Goering's Scandinavian-based aircraft were tried once, but the Me 110s proved insufficiently manoeuvrable to protect bombers.

All the same, the toll of Spitfires mounted, if not in proportion to Messerschmitts. Had Goering continued the assault, he might have achieved air supremacy by sheer numbers. Damage was heavy on the ground, particularly during the fortnight which ended on 6 September. Fighter losses were beginning to outstrip fighter production and another two weeks bombardment of airfields might have turned the tide of victory in favour of Germany. But Churchill, understanding the German mentality better than Goering did the British, decided to bomb Berlin in a daring night raid on 25 August, and this attack continued for several nights thereafter. Although the damage done was minimal and of no military advantage whatever, it had one remarkable result. Hitler and Goering decided to retaliate against British cities. On 7 September 300 bombers of the Luftwaffe attacked London. A thousand people were killed and damage was

Above: *The Old Bailey after a blitz.* Below: *A posed shot of an Me-109 and a Spitfire taken over France as if over Britain.*

heavy. Hitler moved his assault craft to action stations, and Churchill warned the public that a Nazi invasion was imminent on 11 September. But this was Hitler's second and fatal mistake. British morale did not flag; it intensified in the heat of the fires caused by the bombing. And the RAF got another vital breathing space. By choosing to attack cities rather than airfields, Germany lost the Battle of Britain.

The daylight raids hit their peak on 15 September, and 56 German aircraft were lost on that one day alone. Although bombing continued almost until the end of the war, although Coventry was wiped out on 14 November, although the fighting in the skies over England remained intense for months – the Battle of Britain was over. The RAF had not been destroyed. The invasion could not take place. Operation Sea Lion was cancelled on 12 October. Germany lost 1,150 aircraft in the battle; Britain about 650. Both sides over-estimated the enemy losses, but Germany's figure of well over 2,000 British planes destroyed was a more serious miscalculation. The real credit undoubtedly went to the 'few', the fighter pilots of the RAF who worked feverishly, often sixteen hours a day, many of them taking off in new planes the same day they were shot down. The Battle of Britain was the first turning point in the war against Hitler. He had not yet reached the zenith of his power or his conquests; but he had failed to conquer Britain. As Churchill put it: 'Never in the field of human conflict was so much owed by so many to so few.'

Left: Germany's U-boats were the scourge of the Atlantic from the outset of the war until 1943, when Allied counter-measures administered a resounding defeat to Hitler's plans to dominate the Atlantic and cut Britain off from vital supplies. Although they were regrouped and re-equipped, they never again were in a position to win the war by starving Britain into submission.

BATTLE OF THE ATLANTIC

From the first days of the war Britain controlled the vital sea lanes between her islands, the Empire, and the US. Germany's attempt to cut these sea links inaugurated the Battle of the Atlantic.

'Winston is back.' This signal was flashed to the British fleet on 3 September, 1939, after Prime Minister Chamberlain appointed Churchill to the post he had held during World War One – First Lord of the Admiralty. Thanks in part to Churchill's efforts, there was no 'sitzkrieg' at sea. The battle for the control of sea lanes in and out of Britain began as soon as war was declared. Britain's traditional naval supremacy was apparent from the first. Since the German fleet had either been sunk during World War One or scuttled at Scapa Flow in 1919, Germany had been forced to make a fresh start after Hitler seized power in 1933. By 1939 her naval pro-

gramme had only just begun and had not even reached the limits imposed by the Anglo-German Naval Agreement of 1935, which allowed her to construct a fleet of up to 35 per cent of the size of Britain's. On the other hand the German navy was entirely modern. And in the field of submarines the Germans displayed great strength in numbers and skill, remembering that they had almost prevailed in World War One by attacking the shipping which linked Britain with the rest of the world. Nevertheless, the German fleet, whether above or below the high seas, was not as great a challenge to the Royal Navy as it had been in 1914. Despite every effort of interwar British

Above left: Hitler and Admiral Raeder attend the launch of a new warship of the Kriegsmarine. Raeder tried to educate Hitler about the importance of sea power and won support for the creation of a balanced surface and underwater fleet. After the debacle of the Barents Sea action in December 1942, Hitler's threat to dispose of the entire German surface fleet caused Raeder to resign in disgust. Despite his anger, the Führer was persuaded by Raeder's successor, Admiral Doenitz, to retain the surface ships. Below: The British battleship Rodney *fires her 16-inch guns in an exercise after the war broke out. She and her sister ship,* Nelson, *were the most modern ships in the British battle fleet at the start of the war, and they played an active role in the conflict in every theatre of operations throughout the war.*

Above: *The French battleship* Richelieu *had been damaged at Dakar in 1940. After the German occupation of southern France in 1942, she was one of many Vichy French naval units which joined the Allies. She is seen here at Trincomalee in Ceylon after being completely refitted and repaired by the US Navy.* Below: *The stern of the* Bismarck, *showing the colossal beam of this 41,000 ton battleship. With her eight 15-inch guns and her endurance capacity of 10,000 miles, the* Bismarck *could have disrupted the entire Atlantic convoy system long enough to allow the U-boats to win the Battle of the Atlantic. For this reason she was a prime target, and even the loss of HMS* Hood *was a cheap price to pay for the elimination of this massive capital ship.*

Above: *The battleship* Bismarck *refueling at sea from the heavy cruiser* Prinz Eugen *in 1941 before her last sortie.*

governments to reduce expenditure on ships and to dismantle existing bases, the Royal Navy heavily outnumbered the enemy, although it lacked sufficient numbers of naval aircraft. The Swordfish, a cumbersome biplane of antiquated design, not only did remarkable service during the early years of the war, but continued in production through 1945.

The Royal Navy had taken note of the lessons to be learned from the expensive mistakes of World War One. Plans for convoying began well before 1939, for it had been clearly shown in 1917–18 that convoys could successfully resist

Above: *Hitler and Admiral Doenitz, who was a much more politically astute naval officer than Raeder. He consistently promoted the supremacy of the U-boat arm of the Kriegsmarine. When he displaced Raeder circumstances forced him to accept the wisdom of the broad strategy of his predecessor. Doenitz ended the war as the second and last Führer of the Third Reich after Hitler's suicide.*

Above: *Two views of a U-boat under attack from an RAF coastal command Sunderland flying boat. From 1942 aircraft played an increasingly important part in overcoming the submarine threat, and by 1945 had sunk more U-boats than had been sunk by all other methods.* Below: *The pocket battleship* Graf Spee *was reduced to a blazing wreck in the River Plate by her own crew. Hitler preferred the disgrace of scuttling to the capture or defeat in battle of his prize ocean raider. He ordered the destruction of the* Graf Spee *after she was cornered by three British cruisers near Montevideo.*

submarines if organized in sufficient numbers. Thus, despite some early losses to U-boats, the British effectively commanded the seas around their islands from the very beginning of the war. By October some 3,600 mines had been laid in the Dover Straits. This led the Germans to concentrate on the North Sea and the waters around Scotland, but the toll in precious U-boats was heavy. By March 1940 they had lost one-third of their submarines, and only eleven new ones had been commissioned. Admittedly, Britain had lost 222 ships at a rate of some 100,000 tons per month since the start of the war, but German magnetic mines rather than subs were largely responsible for these losses. After one such mine, dropped on land, was captured and dissected, countermeasures were taken which rendered this 'secret' weapon far less effective.

As in World War One, Germany had to challenge the Royal Navy directly in order to win control of the North Sea. On 8 October, 1939, the battle cruiser *Gneisenau* and the light cruiser *Köln* sailed into the North Sea, and Britain sent the battleship *Royal Oak* to meet them. The Germans fled back to Kiel, but later U-47 sent the giant British ship to the bottom of Scapa Flow. In another uneven skirmish the *Gneisenau* and the *Scharnhorst* sank the British armed merchant liner *Rawalpindi,* after the latter put up a heroic struggle. But these adventures only pointed out the fundamental weakness of the German Navy. It could attack and run; it could hit single ships in a U-boat raid; but it could not afford to stand and fight in numbers. Rather than risk another Jutland, with predictably disastrous results, the Germans chose to raid and harass. And the German ship which was most successful in eluding the Royal Navy was the *Graf Spee*.

Graf Spee was a pocket battleship which had both great speed and excellent firepower. In October Britain and France sent out eight groups to hunt down the *Graf Spee* which by now had claimed nine ships in the Southern Hemisphere. In mid-December the cruiser HMS *Exeter* caught her off the coast of Argentina, near the mouth of the River Plate. *Exeter* was badly damaged in the first skirmish, but the cruisers *Ajax* and *Achilles* then hit Captain Hans Langsdorff's ship so hard that she had to put into the neutral port of Montevideo, Uruguay. Commodore Henry Harwood let it be known that the carrier *Ark Royal* and the battle cruiser *Renown* were waiting offshore, even though they were thousands of miles away. Obliged to leave the port within 72 hours, Langsdorff let his crew disembark and sailed off in the company of a German merchant ship. On the evening of 17 December he scuttled *Graf Spee* before the British could reach her, and two days later shot himself. Although strategically of little significance, the sinking of *Graf Spee* was a timely moral victory which caught the imagination of the British public, only just beginning to awaken to the fact that the nation was in grave danger and was, after all, at war.

There was a sequel to the episode as well. Captain Langsdorff had transferred the crews of his victims to the armed tanker *Altmark*, which then headed for Norway. On 17 February, 1940,

British forces boarded *Altmark* within Norwegian territorial waters and rescued the prisoners held on her. This was another moral victory at sea which intensified British public opinion against Germany. Clearly the old lion of the seas was beginning to show its teeth.

Britain retained command of the seas throughout the disaster of the western blitzkrieg, the Dunkirk evacuation and the scuttling of the French fleet after the fall of France. This attack, designed to prevent the huge French Navy from falling into German hands, was led by *Ark Royal* and the battle cruiser *Hood.* Although almost 1,300 Frenchmen died at Mers-el Kebir on 3 July, 1940, the British eliminated a major potential threat, despite the fact that twelve French ships, including the battle cruiser *Strasbourg,* eluded capture or destruction. The new battleship *Richelieu* escaped as well at Dakar, but the operation was, on the whole, an important success. Hitler's plans to invade Britain were partially thwarted at Mers-el-Kebir.

On 17 August, 1940, Hitler ordered a complete blockade of British coasts. It was a threat he was incapable of carrying out, but nevertheless illegal so long as neutral ships bound for Britain did not carry contraband. One consequence was that the United States traded 50 over-age destroyers in exchange for bases in the Western Hemisphere, thus easing British supply problems during the Battle of Britain. By the end of 1940 Germany had lost 31 submarines and had only 22 left, which virtually cleared the Atlantic. The Lend-Lease Act, which came into force in early 1941, effectively allowed the US to give Britain massive financial and naval support, which was underlined in September 1941 when President Roosevelt ordered American ships challenged by U-boats to shoot on sight. Thus the US gave Britain as much naval assistance as she could short of declaring war outright. The British Isles were safe from the slow torture of blockade as well as from direct invasion from the Continent.

But the Atlantic naval war was far from over. On 5 November, 1940, the pocket battleship *Scheer* sank the armed merchant cruiser *Jervis Bay* and sixteen other ships; and the cruiser *Hipper* took a toll of seven ships from a convoy in 1941. The U-boats came out again in the spring of 1941 after *Scharnhorst* and *Gneisenau* had temporarily been put out of action by the RAF. By now Germany had up to 40 submarines which continued to harass shipping, but she was losing them faster than she could build them and her days of commerce raiding were almost over. In May 1941 Admiral Lütjens' great new battleship *Bismarck* and the cruiser *Prinz Eugen* sailed from German-occupied Poland pursued by the battleship *Prince of Wales,* four destroyers, and the battle cruiser *Hood.* On 23 May they were sighted in the Denmark Strait between Greenland and Iceland. In the ensuing battle *Hood* was sunk. *Prince of Wales* was hit, but managed to damage the *Bismarck* in the process, forcing Lütjens to turn back in the direction of the French coast. During the Germans' escape a Swordfish hit the *Bismarck* with a torpedo. The battleship continued on her way although now separated from

the *Prinz Eugen*. The cordon of British ships tightened and eventually the *Bismarck* was spotted only some 30 hours from Brest and safety. *Ark Royal* now joined the hunt. On 27 May the battleships *King George V* and *Rodney* closed in and hit her with everything they had. The *Bismarck* sank with colours flying less than two hours later, almost 2,000 members of her crew going down with her.

The sinking of the *Bismarck* was the last major battle between the British and German navies in the war. But the U-boat campaign intensified as production reached 40 per month in 1942. Although Hitler was by now obsessed with his war in the East against Russia, Admiral Doenitz sent his submarines far and wide to attack Allied shipping, inflicting severe losses in the Far East during the early months of the war against Japan. As America strengthened forces in the Pacific, Britain was obliged to help protect the East Coast of the United States and the U-boats reaped a rich harvest, sinking over three million tons of ships in the first six months of 1942, the year in which the Allies lost more ships than ever before – 1664, of which over 1100 were accounted for by submarines. But by early 1943 the Battle of the Atlantic was won. Allied convoy systems were perfected and Germany's naval victories thereafter were confined largely to the Indian Ocean, far from the main lines of shipping. The *Scharn-*

Top left: *The British merchantman* Coulmore *wallowing in an Atlantic storm. Bad weather conditions made station keeping extremely difficult for ships in convoy, but it also inhibited the activities of U-boats.* Left: *Crewmen of the US Coast Guard cutter* Spencer *watch a salvo of depth charges exploding during an Atlantic convoy battle.* Below left: *German heavy warships in the Arctic attempted to cut off Allied supplies to the Soviet Union who depended heavily in 1941–2 on Allied shipments of food and munitions to their northern ports of Archangel and Murmansk.* Below: *The shattered conning tower of a U-boat seen from a hostile aircraft.*

Above: *HMS* Hood *was launched in 1918 and is seen here on her builders' trials in 1920. As Admiral Somerville's flagship she fired on the French fleet at Mers-el-Kebir in 1940 and was sunk by the* Bismarck *in May 1941.* Below: *The American tanker* Dixie Arrow *was sunk off the East Coast of the US in 1942, one of the many casualties inflicted by German U-boats in their onslaught on unprotected American shipping.*

Above: *From the end of 1942 the Allies organized support groups consisting of at least one escort carrier and a number of escorts. These groups operated independently either hunting submarines or coming to the aid of convoys.*

Above: *The US Navy's answer to the submarine threat was to place orders for more than a thousand destroyer-escorts (DEs). From the end of 1942 these began to come forward in increasing numbers. USS* Fiske *(DE 143) is seen here as a twisted wreck after being hit by a submarine torpedo, launched by U-804 north of the Azores on 2 August 1944.*

Above: *The US Coast Guard provided invaluable reinforcements of trained seamen and ships to the US Navy in the Battle of the Atlantic. Cutters like the* Duane *seen here in heavy seas in 1943, were converted to heavily armed escorts with little trouble and proved to be as efficient as regular anti-submarine escorts.*

horst was destroyed off the North Cape in December 1943. The *Tirpitz* was badly damaged in April 1944 in a Norwegian fjord, and was finally destroyed by aerial attack in November of the same year with almost 1,000 men trapped in her when she turned over. Even the convoy route to Russia was now secured.

The U-boats fought on to the bitter end. Although their numbers reached an all-time peak in March 1945 (463), and they continued to create occasional havoc, sea lanes were effectively clear for the rest of the war. Altogether 1,162 German submarines were at sea at one time or another, and 785 were destroyed. Some 2,800 Allied or neutral ships were lost to submarines throughout the war. But the cost to Germany was high. Most of her merchant fleet was destroyed by Allied ships, planes and mines, and in the course of the war she lost effective commercial contact with the non-European world. The war at sea was as vicious as it was terrifying. To give some indication of German ferocity, over half the surviving German submarines refused to capitulate at the end of the war and scuttled themselves. But the Battle of the Atlantic pointed up Allied naval supremacy throughout the war. Hitler underestimated both the importance of naval power and the strength of British determination to fight once called upon to do so – a fact which made a great deal of difference to the German war effort.

Top: *A Swordfish takes off from a British carrier in the Med.*
Above: *British naval forces approach the port of Piraeus led by*
HMS Orion *under Captain Mansfield. They were to help in the*
defence of Greece after the German attempt to aid Italy.

MISADVENTURE

Italy stumbled into attacking Greece in 1940, but within a week Mussolini's armies were in retreat. Germany came to its Axis partner's aid, bringing about and completing a full-scale invasion of the Balkans before beginning the invasion of Russia.

Up to the end of summer 1940 Hitler's Italian ally had remained in the war's shadows, first by choice, then by circumstances. Mussolini's inglorious intervention in France earned him little applause and much criticism at home. Il Duce needed a victory. He chose Greece as a suitable victim. Germany would find it difficult to interfere, Britain was fighting for her life and could not give much help, and besides, Italy had 45 million people and Greece only seven million. To Mussolini it seemed a good match.

In August 1940 Italy requested Greece to renounce the guarantee which Britain had given King George of the Hellenes and his quasi-dictator, General Metaxas, in 1939. Greece refused and the Italian army mobilized in Albania. An ultimatum was delivered to Greece on the evening of 27–28 October as Italian troops crossed the Greek frontier. But Greek resistance was unexpectedly tough. The three divisions involved in the attack were hurled back within a week, and soon Greek troops were advancing into Italian Albania. Britain set up RAF stations in Crete and on 11 November hammered three

Italian battleships in a night raid on the southern port of Taranto, forcing the Italians to abandon it as a base and to operate only from west coast ports. This development gave the RAF ample opportunity to attack Rumanian oil fields from the same bases in Crete. By now things were going badly for Mussolini in the North African desert campaign he had begun in September 1940. But they were far worse in the Balkans. By December there were no more Italian troops on Greek soil. A quarter of Albania was in Greek hands; and Valona, Albania's principal port, was being attacked.

Matters had gone far enough for Hitler. Obliged to help his ally in the Pact of Steel, he now planned a build-up in the Balkans for a spring offensive. Meanwhile, British planes bombarded Leghorn and Spezia while British ships hammered Genoa. British forces moved into Italian Somaliland and Ethiopia, and Hitler was forced to prop up Italy's sagging defences in the Desert War by sending in Erwin Rommel and the Afrika Korps. On 28 March, 1941 British naval superiority in the Mediterranean was

Left: *Benito Mussolini, Il Duce, Italy's dictator since 1922.* Above: *HMS* Warspite, *a veteran of the Battle of Jutland in World War I, at anchor in Malta after the Battle of Matapan, which underlined British naval supremacy in the Mediterranean in 1941.*

dramatically affirmed at the Battle of Matapan, where three Italian cruisers and two destroyers were sunk. Despite the fact that the main target, the battleship *Vittorio Veneto* got away, the Italian Navy was no longer a factor in the war. Hitler had formed a Tripartite Pact with Italy and Japan in September 1940. Rumania had joined the so-called Axis in November and in March 1941 Bulgaria and Yugoslavia were also forced to join. All was in readiness for Germany to plunge into Greece when Yugoslavia overthrew the government of Prince Paul on 27 March. This stroke of good fortune for Britain compelled Hitler to change his plans once again – instead of attacking Greece at leisure through Bulgaria, German troops would have to strike against both Yugoslavia and Greece. These delays gave Britain an opportunity to land troops in Greece proper – an error of judgement if not of sympathy, since there was little she could do to stop a Nazi attack.

On 6 April, 33 German divisions entered Yugoslavia. The Luftwaffe met no effective opposition and in less than a fortnight the country capitulated. Simultaneously Germany pushed into Greece from Bulgaria. It was left to Italy to dispose of the Greeks in Albania. British and Greek forces were inexorably pushed back southwards as the Germans continued their thrust through Yugoslavia and invaded Greece through that country as well. Serbia became a puppet state of the Third Reich. Croatia was made into an 'independent' protectorate. Hungary, Bulgaria and Italy helped themselves to further pieces of the Yugoslav state, and the Allied front in the south began to collapse despite fierce heroic fighting by the Greeks. British, Australian and New Zealand troops began to evacuate Greece; some 43,000 made it; about 11,000 did not. Athens was taken on 27 April and by the end of the month resistance ceased. The whole of the

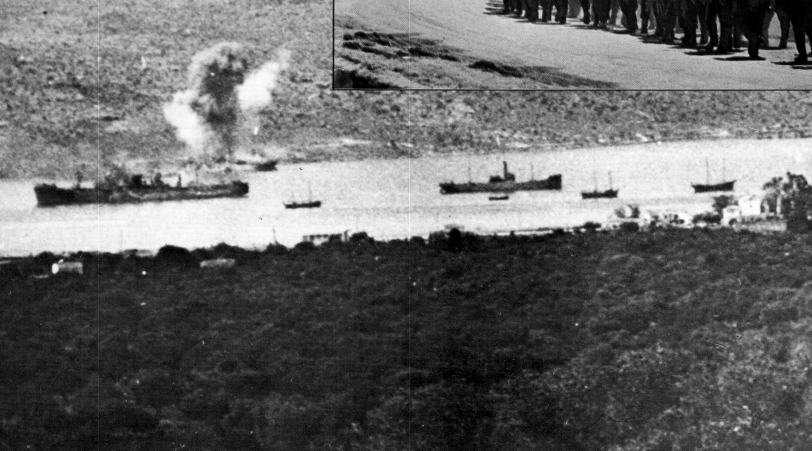

German Invasion and dates of capture 8.4.41

German parachute and airborne landings in Crete 20 May, 1941

British evacuation

YUGOSLAVIA
8.4.41
Skopje

Kyustendil

R Maritza   Plordir

BULGARIA

R.Vardar   Veles
6.4.41

Struma

Prilep

Monastir

R Arda
Nevrokop
Nestos

R. Meric

Florina

Xanthi

Alexandroupolis

Kozani
17.4.41

Thessalonilci
9.4.41

Limnos

TURKEY

Platamon
16.4.41

Lesbos

P Pinios

GREECE

Khios

Thermopylae
24.4.41

Patrai
Corinth
26.4.41

Athens
27.4.41

Aegean Sea

Pirgos

Navplion

Naxos

Kalamata
28.4.41

Ionian Sea

Maleme

28/29.5.41

Rethimnon

Heraklion

Sfakia

CRETE

28.5–1.6.41

Top left: *Italian troops plunge into Greece. Their abortive attack soon turned into headlong retreat.* Top right: *A Greek general discusses surrender terms with a German officer in Athens.* Far left: *A German column of infantry passes through the Rhodope Mountains as it advances from Bulgaria into northern Greece.* Above left: *Some Greek prisoners of war pass German armoured cars on their way into captivity.* Below: *British ships in the Cretan harbour of Suda Bay are hit by German planes.*

Balkans, except for European Turkey (neutral throughout the war) was in German hands.

However, the King of Greece moved his government to Crete to continue the conflict. About 27,000 troops from Greece were assembled there, including the 2nd New Zealand Division and part of the 6th Australian Division. General Sir Archibald Wavell was in charge of the defence of Crete and its strategic airfields. Hitler had to eliminate them to secure his oil refineries in Rumania, and General Kurt Student prepared his aerial assault of the island – the most massive German airborne attack of the entire war. On 20 May glider and parachute landings began. Although Greek airfields on the island were too rough for immediate use by the Luftwaffe, the Germans' seizure of Maleme airfield at the western end of Crete provided a vital base from which to attack the rest of the island more effectively. Because of British naval superiority in the Mediterranean, a seaborne invasion was not possible, but the Luftwaffe commanded the air completely, making short work of two cruisers and three destroyers of the Royal Navy that were protecting the island. Within a week of the German attack the question facing British commanders was how to evacuate the garrison to Egypt.

Britain's failure to recapture Maleme cost her Crete. Over 30,000 British, Greek and Commonwealth troops were unable to hold an island against a far smaller German strike force which could not gain control of the surrounding seas. On 29 May the evacuation began. About 15,000 men escaped; the rest went into POW camps. But the cost of victory was high. Germany lost 220 planes and a third of the men used in the assault. No parachute attack of this type was ever attempted again, and the Germans ruefully concluded afterwards that the seizure of Crete was not worth the effort. The proposed invasion of the vital British base of Malta, which continued to be battered from the air, was abandoned by Hitler. But blitzkrieg tactics had worked once again. Within weeks Germany had taken the Balkans. Fortress Europe was safely in the hands of the Third Reich.

It has often been argued that the Balkan adventure delayed the German attack on the Soviet Union, Operation Barbarossa, and that Moscow and Russia were saved when Hitler was obliged to pull Mussolini's irons out of the fire. This thesis cannot be defended, as Hitler in any event was forced to delay his attack on the USSR until 22 June because of unfavourable weather conditions. The parachute troops would not have been used at all in Russia, and the planes could have been shifted north at short notice. Even the heavy German losses in the air over Crete could be made up by aircraft production in a couple of weeks. Only the tanks used in the Balkan campaign needed a rest and partial refit, but this break was achieved when Greece fell in late April.

The Balkan blitzkrieg was a qualified success for the Third Reich. Now all eyes turned to the East, where Hitler prepared to launch his most audacious campaign yet.

Left: *Luftwaffe passes in triumph over the Parthenon and Acropolis in Athens.*

Above: *Hitler's Panzer divisions swept through White Russia towards Moscow before he ordered a halt to their rapid progress.*
Above right: *German motorcyclists check their maps before they move forward again.* Centre bottom: *Soldiers of the Wehrmacht pause during their rapid advance through the Soviet Union during the summer of 1941.*

OPERATION BARBAROSSA

Charles XII of Sweden had failed to conquer Russia in the 18th century. Napoleon had failed in the 19th century. Hitler felt he could succeed where others had failed. France had collapsed within six weeks. Most foreign observers predicted a Russian collapse within weeks as well, basing their opinions on the Soviet Union's poor performance against Finland in 1939–40. Hitler's generals were not so certain, but on 22 June 1941 Operation Barbarossa was launched.

The German–Soviet pact had served its purpose for two years. In the intervening period Germany had taken over the continent of Europe. Russia had absorbed part of Finland, the three Baltic states, and about one third of Poland. In 1940 she took Bessarabia from Rumania. Russia's officer corps, devastated by Stalin's purges in the 1930s, had been reorganized, with Marshal Semen K. Timoshenko at its head. General Georgi Zhukov was named Chief of Staff, after having conducted a highly successful campaign during the late 1930s against the Japanese in the undeclared war on the borders of Manchukuo. But the changeover to the T-34 tank was not yet complete. Divisions were below strength, and tank corps had not been formed. Stalin was still not ready for the war with Germany which he considered inevitable. He had no faith in Japan with whom he had signed a non-aggression pact in April 1941, and was forced to maintain many divisions in the Far East in case she planned a double-cross. His armies were loosely strung out along Russia's long western frontier, and he needed and expected more time to prepare.

Although Russia had 20,000 tanks, most of them were obsolete. Her air force was sufficiently large, her rate of production having been stepped up steadily to surpass that of Germany. By June 1941 Russia was building 1,000 planes a month. But no reserve force existed, supplies of fuel were short, and pilots were untrained. Above all, the Russian fighters were slower than the Me 109s. The Soviet Union's great strength was in manpower – twelve million, including reserves, under arms. Germany's boast that the whole rotten edifice of Communism would come crashing down within weeks was, to say the least, optimistic.

Germany had her problems too. Of her 205 divisions, 60 were obliged to occupy and police territory so recently conquered. She had failed to end the war with Britain, and her soldiers were now committed to the Western Desert. She was losing the war at sea. Hitler's intention had been first to destroy Britain and then turn on the Soviet Union. Now his plan was to defeat Russia quickly and then finish off the UK. The Pzkw IV tanks had not been produced in sufficient num-

Above right: *Stukas at a Luftwaffe base in Bulgaria, a forward staging area for Operation Barbarossa.* Below left: *German artillery men move into position as their advance continues.* Below right: *General Friedrich von Manstein was promoted to the rank of Field Marshal when his XI Army took Sebastopol in the Crimea after an arduous fight.*

bers, so that many older models had not yet been replaced. Furthermore, many of the vehicles now being produced in French factories were unsuited to Russian climatic conditions. Overconfidence was to prove Germany's worst enemy. Chief of Staff General Franz Halder estimated victory within eight to ten weeks. The British Embassy in Moscow suggested only six. Hitler believed that four might be enough. His army was not even equipped with winter clothing, although the Waffen-SS and the Luftwaffe showed more perspicacity.

Hitler's plunge into Russia on 22 June, 1941 caught Stalin by surprise, despite repeated warnings that an attack was at hand. Frontier defences were quickly overrun, as the Germans attacked in three directions: Army Group South headed for the Ukraine; Centre for Moscow; and North for Leningrad. This was Hitler's last blitzkrieg. Everything depended on yet another easy and swift victory. At first all seemed to go remarkably well. Army Group North, under Field Marshal Wilhelm von Leeb, pressed into Lithuania toward Leningrad, which by October was under heavy siege. Army Group Centre, under Field Marshal von Bock, took Brest-Litovsk and reached Smolensk by 16 July. Army Group South, under Field Marshal von Rundstedt, advanced toward Kiev. The Russians hoped to stem the Nazi tide at the Stalin Line, which stretched from the Estonian frontier to west of Kiev. This line could not be held, but by this time Hitler's concept of the attack was altering weekly. First he proclaimed Leningrad his main target; then, Moscow; then, Kiev and the Ukraine. After German troops breached the Stalin Line on 12 July, he decided to concentrate on the south, holding up Bock's forces in the centre for two crucial months on the Desna. On 21 August he ordered the seizure of Kiev. General Guderian's Panzers were taken from Bock for this purpose, while General Hermann Hoth's Panzers were sent north to help Leeb take Leningrad. The Kiev encirclement was a great success. The two German pincers met 150 miles to the east of the city, trapping 600,000 Russian troops in the process. Aided by the errors of Marshal Budenny, who was relieved of his command, Kiev fell on 18 September. But a shadow hung over the German victory. Winter was setting in. Roads were becoming impassable. Hitler, now realizing that this war would take longer than he contemplated, ordered Army Group Centre to advance, after long delay, towards Moscow.

Bock won initial success. A further 600,000 Russians were captured around Vyasma in October, but winter was tightening its grip. Snow fell and the unpaved Russian roads became a morass of mud, then ice. Hitler's generals advised him to form a line of defence for the rest of the winter, as the German troops were tired after an advance of well over a thousand miles on all three fronts. But the Führer, convinced that a stalemate would produce a compromise peace, ordered the troops to press forward. Bock resumed the push towards Moscow on 15 November when the weather improved. By early December the Germans were within 20 miles of Moscow, entering its suburbs. But by now the temperature had fallen below zero Fahrenheit, and heavy snow halted the advance. The effect on the German soldiers, without winter clothing, was devastating. Hitler had lost his chance of taking Moscow by pausing to hold the centre in August. Now it was too late. While Joseph Goebbels, back in Germany, was organizing the collection of winter clothing for the troops, Zhukov launched a counter-attack on 6 December. Remembering Napoleon's disastrous winter of 1812, Hitler refused to permit a withdrawal. This time he was right, and German lines held. But Moscow was still in Russian hands.

In the south the Crimea was taken, and Rostov was captured, but a Russian counter-thrust pushed the Germans out again. Rundstedt suggested a withdrawal to a line of defence along the Mius River, but Hitler forbade it – unwisely. Rundstedt resigned, Russian troops advanced, and Hitler was forced to order a retreat after all. When Leeb suggested a strategic withdrawal from Leningrad for the winter, and Hitler refused, he too resigned. So did Bock, after Zhukov's counter-attack. Guderian was fired for withdrawing his men, despite Hitler's orders to the contrary. Finally Field Marshal Walther von Brauchitsch, Commander-in-Chief of the German Army, resigned officially for reasons of ill health. Thus all Hitler's top commanders, many of them the agents of his greatest victories, were replaced in December, with one exception – Brauchitsch. Hitler himself took over his job as Commander-in-Chief.

The line was held by freezing, exhausted soldiers. However, Russian losses had been tremendous – at least three million men and about 18,000 tanks during the first three months of

Above: *Horses of the Wehrmacht pause for a drink during the Barbarossa offensive. Much of the German artillery was still horse-drawn in 1941.*
Below: *Exhausted motor cyclists pause as the German thrust into Russia taxed their physical endurance.*

Above: *The summer of 1941 was a victorious holiday for soldiers of the Wehrmacht. The holiday came to an abrupt end when the Russians dug in before Moscow and Leningrad.*

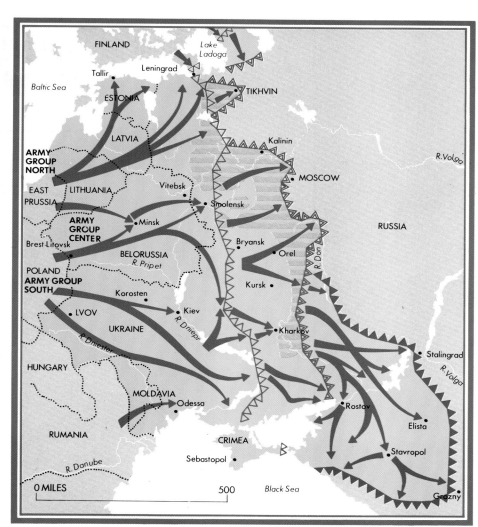

Axis Powers advance into Russia

22 June–1 Sept 1941

1 Sept–5 Dec 1941

Reoccupied by Russians during counterattack, 6 Dec 1941–April 1942

Further advance in the South 28 June–18 Nov 1942 (Regaining some of the ground lost in 41/42 winter campaign)

Left: *Infantrymen cross a river without encountering any Soviet opposition in the early stages of the march into the Ukraine. The opposition became fierce as winter set in.*

Above and right: *German columns sweep through Russian towns on the road to Moscow.*

Barbarossa. But the edifice had not crumbled. Hitler had made his second great error and met with his second great failure. First England was not taken; now Russia. It was to be his fatal blunder. He had always relied on short campaigns and rapid successes. If he could not defeat Russia quickly, he could never win.

Although December 1941 looked dark for Hitler, the Allies were still to suffer further losses. Stalin learned from his agent in Tokyo, Richard Sorge, that Japan planned to attack in the Pacific. But neither he, nor Franklin D. Roosevelt, President of the United States, knew where the attack would occur. The world found out on the morning of 7 December, 1941. The targets were Malaya, the Philippines, the Dutch East Indies – and Pearl Harbor, Hawaii.

Below: *A wrecked Russian tank seems to be saluted by a statue of Lenin in a town occupied by the Nazis.*

DISASTER IN THE PACIFIC

President Roosevelt provoked the Japanese to attack in the Pacific when the US, Britain and the Netherlands froze Japanese assets on 26 June 1941. Japan was obliged to withdraw from China or wage war against the West. An attack was expected, but it was assumed that it would be on the Philippines or even Malaya. It was not expected at Pearl Harbor, Hawaii. On the morning of 7 December 1941, the Japanese Zeros shocked America into action.

Japan's march of empire began in 1895 when she defeated China. Her victory against Russia in 1905, her gains at the expense of Germany in World War One, and her seizure of Manchuria in 1931 only whetted her appetite for what Foreign Minister Matsuoka later called a Greater East Asia Co-Prosperity Sphere. In 1937 Japan entered China proper, conquering most of her coastline and many of her largest cities. The United States thanks to the spirit of isolationism which was the legacy of disillusionment with World War One, made no effective response. Although the US did place an embargo on the shipment of high-octane petroleum and scrap steel after Japan seized part of French Indo-China in late 1940, she did not take decisive action until after the rest of Indo-China was taken in July 1941. By then the destroyer-base deal, Lend-Lease and other non-neutral acts had ended any pretence that America was disinterested in the outcome of the war in Europe. On 26 July, 1941, the US along with Britain and the Dutch government-in-exile in London, froze Japanese assets held in their banks. This forced Japan either to wage war on a wider scale in the Far East or withdraw from her continuing war in China – a domestically unacceptable alternative. Unable to draw the reluctant American people into the war in Europe (despite the seizure of Greenland and Iceland by American forces in 1941, and the shoot-on-sight order in the Atlantic) President Roosevelt hoped to provoke an attack in the Pacific, assuming that the US could somehow become directly involved in supporting Britain's and Russia's struggle against Nazism.

Top left: *The* USS Maryland *in the background, and boats from the overturned* USS Oklahoma *in the foreground, after the Pearl Harbor attack.*
Top centre: *Japanese view of Pearl Harbor just before 0800 when the strike force swept through the mountain pass on Oahu and sighted the flotilla anchored at Pearl. The exploding shells in the background were the first shots fired in the war in the Pacific.* Top right: *A bombadier's view of Battleship Row on Pearl Harbor Day, a day which Roosevelt proclaimed 'would live in infamy' in his speech the following day when he asked the Congress to declare war on Japan.*
Right: *Pearl Harbor under attack as seen from the tail end of Battleship Row. Much of the Pacific Fleet was destroyed on the morning of 7 December, 1941 except vital aircraft carriers.*

Above: *HMS* Prince of Wales *and* Repulse *after being hit by Japanese torpedoes off Kirantan, 10 December 1941. Churchill had sent these two capital ships to the Far East to bolster the defences of Singapore but insufficient air cover made them sitting targets for the Zekes and Zeros of the Japanese air force. A British destroyer is seen in the foreground.*

Above: *Captured Americans and Filipinos after the fall of Corregidor. They were forced to march to POW camps in what has been called 'The Death March'. Thousands fell by the wayside, parched for water and starved of food. Those who could not make it were either left to die or were shot on the spot.* Above right: *British defenders of Hong Kong are marched into captivity. Hong Kong fell after a heroic defence on Christmas Day 1941.*

Above: *The Japanese attack on the Philippines coincided with the blitz on Pearl Harbor. Government buildings in Manila are under attack as MacArthur was obliged to retreat to the Bataan peninsula, where American and Filipino forces were besieged.*

Above: *USS* Pope *under fire from Japanese heavy cruisers off Java.*

Above: *Wounded from the USS* Marblehead *are unloaded at Tjilatjap, Java, in the Dutch East Indies after the Battle of the Java Sea (27–28 February 1942). In just over a week the entire Dutch East Indies had fallen to Japan. The USS* Houston *is shown in the background.*

Above: *Japanese soldiers march into Singapore after its surrender, the most ignominious display of irresolution in the history of Britain at war.*

The opportunity presented itself with a vengeance on the morning of 7 December.

On the date that Roosevelt said would 'live in infamy', Japanese aircraft attacked and destroyed 349 American planes, not more than a dozen of which were able to take off from Hickam Field near Pearl Harbor. The US suffered well over 3,000 casualties and lost three battleships, three light cruisers and three destroyers. Four other battleships were badly damaged. But fortunately no aircraft carrier, the principal weapon in World War Two in the Pacific, was hit. They were all out at sea on missions. The next day the United States declared war against Japan. For once as good as their word, Hitler and Mussolini declared war on the United States on 11 December. The various conflicts being fought around the world were joined, and the first truly global conflict in human history had begun. Now the world's greatest industrial power was ranged on the side of Britain and Russia against Germany, Italy and Japan.

Japan had dealt a humiliating blow to the Americans. But it was by no means a mortal thrust. She never planned to follow up the Pearl Harbor attack by a landing; nor did she destroy the oil stocks on the island of Oahu. The Japanese plan was to knock the US out of the Pacific war at a stroke while seizing the valuable petroleum supplies of the Dutch East Indies as well as the rice, rubber and tin of Southeast Asia. The first hundred days were an unmitigated truimph. Japan swept through the Far East like an uncontrollable tropical storm. Armed with aircraft carriers, her fleet air arm destroyed the British battleship *Prince of Wales* and the battle cruiser *Repulse,* which had no air cover, in the first days of the war. Guam was overrun on 10 December; Wake Island on the 23rd. Hong Kong fell on Christmas Day. As Japanese troops swept down the Malay Peninsula in tanks, on foot and on bicycles, Britain prepared for the defence of its great fortress in the Far East – Singapore. Landings on Luzon in the Philippines forced General Douglas MacArthur to evacuate the capital city of Manila on the 27 December. By January MacArthur's back was to the wall with 40,000 men in the Bataan Peninsula, and General A. E. Percival was beginning his ill-considered preparations for Singapore. Japan took Kuala Lumpur on 10 January. Percival, and Churchill, to his horror, realized that some of the guns of the fortifications for the island stronghold were pointing out to sea. Japan was attacking from the landward side. Percival had to alter his defence plans.

General Tomoyuki Yamashita's forces advanced steadily down the Malay Peninsula, but with insufficient troops to take Singapore easily. They had not expected British complacency. Reinforcements had been sent to Singapore to defend the island fortress. But they never got the opportunity to fight the enemy. Instead of fighting on in the spirit of the Battle of Britain or Dunkirk, Percival yielded Singapore despite the fact that his troops outnumbered those of Japan. He had organized no clear pattern of defence and he did not offer even a face-saving resistance;

Above: *The British surrender at Singapore, the blackest day for British arms in World War II.* Below: *The Japanese enter Mandalay. Burma fell almost as quickly as Malaya, and the British fell back to India to defend their Asian Empire.*

merely meek surrender of 85,000 men once the Japanese had crossed the causeway from Johore and had landed on the the island. The Japanese bluffed the British and had pulled it off. The fall of Singapore on 15 February, 1942, was one of the most humiliating episodes in the annals of British military history.

The same could not be said of Bataan and Corregidor in the Philippines. MacArthur's exhausted army of Filipinos and Americans held out bravely against hopeless odds for months. MacArthur was ordered to leave Bataan by Roosevelt in late February; on 11 March his flotilla of four speed-boats ran the Japanese blockade, and MacArthur escaped to Australia, promising that he would return to liberate the island colony which he had grown to love. General Jonathan Wainwright valiantly held out for another month; and when Bataan fell on 9 April he and his beleaguered men defended the rock of Corregidor Island until its inevitable capture on 6 May. Wainwright and his troops were then herded into captivity on the 'death march' when those who did not die of dysentery, hunger and exhaustion survived only to face maltreatment at the hands of the Japanese special police, the Kempeitai. Wainwright emerged a living skeleton at the end of the war.

Given permission to pass through Thailand, Japanese troops entered Burma on 11 December. Here too the British were complacent, believing, despite the Malayan experience, that tanks could not penetrate jungle. Rangoon fell on 1 March, and the arrival of Nationalist Chinese troops to aid the British did not make much difference. The Japanese advanced up-country and by mid-May the whole of Burma was in their hands, despite brilliant rearguard actions in the face of disaster by Lt. General William Slim. British forces retired to India. In the Far East only the mountain fastnesses of Chiang Kai-shek's corrupt Nationalist Chinese regime purported to hold out against Japan, as well as Mao Tse-tung's Communists, who maintained their control over parts of north-western China.

The Empire of Japan spread southwards. Once Singapore had fallen, the Dutch in the East Indies had little hope of resisting the imperial wave. Their outer islands were overrun early in the war, but in stubborn Dutch fashion, their small navy, helped by some American and Australian ships, decided to go down with flags flying in the Battle of the Java Sea (27-28 February). They fought well and bravely, but the outcome was inevitable. Java was occupied and the Dutch ceased fire on 9 March. Their extraordinary Governor-General, Tjarda van Starkenborgh-Stachouwer, chose captivity along with his people rather than escape to Australia. Some 250,000 Dutch and Indo-Europeans spent the rest of the war in concentration camps as guests of the Kempeitai.

The whole of South-East Asia was conquered in the first hundred days or so of the Pacific war. India and Australia lay open to aerial attack. Not satisfied with this incredible triumph, however, Japan pressed westward and southward. The line of defence had still to be drawn.

Above: *Union Jacks fly at the frontier railway bridge near Moulmein, Burma as the first Japanese soldiers approach the frontier from Thailand at the start of the invasion of Burma.*

Above: *Japanese infantrymen in Java during the occupation of the Dutch East Indies. The cease fire was initialled on 9 March, 1942. Above right: General Hideki Tojo, Prime Minister and supreme warlord of Japan, who came to office weeks before Pearl Harbor. He made the final decision with Imperial Consent to attack the possessions of the US, Britain and the Netherlands in the Pacific. Below: Japanese troops in Malaya. Their plunge down the Malay peninsula was swift. Within a month they were putting pressure on Singapore at the southern tip of the peninsula, where they expected a stout defence from the British.*

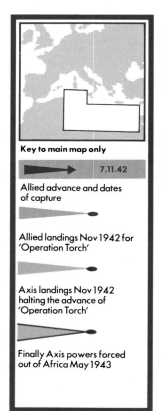

Key to main map only

7.11.42

Allied advance and dates of capture

Allied landings Nov 1942 for 'Operation Torch'

Axis landings Nov 1942 halting the advance of 'Operation Torch'

Finally Axis powers forced out of Africa May 1943

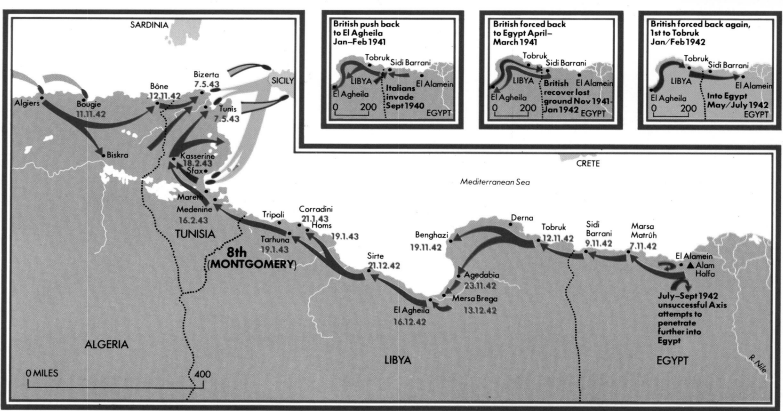

SARDINIA

SICILY

Algiers

Bougie
11.11.42

Bône
12.11.42

Bizerta
7.5.43

Tunis
7.5.43

Biskra

Kasserine
18.2.43

Sfax

Mareth

Medenine
16.2.43

TUNISIA

8th (MONTGOMERY)

Tripoli

Tarhuna
19.1.43

Corradini
21.1.43

Homs
19.1.43

Sirte
21.12.42

El Agheila
16.12.42

Mersa Brega
13.12.42

Agedabia
23.11.42

Benghazi
19.11.42

Derna

Tobruk
12.11.42

Sidi Barrani
9.11.42

Marsa Matrûh
7.11.42

El Alamein
▲ Alam Halfa

Mediterranean Sea

CRETE

July–Sept 1942 unsuccessful Axis attempts to penetrate further into Egypt

ALGERIA

LIBYA

EGYPT

R. Nile

0 MILES   400

British push back to El Agheila Jan–Feb 1941

Tobruk Sidi Barrani

LIBYA El Alamein

El Agheila **Italians invade Sept 1940**

0   200   EGYPT

British forced back to Egypt April– March 1941

Tobruk Sidi Barrani

LIBYA El Alamein

El Agheila **British recover lost ground Nov 1941– Jan 1942**

0   200   EGYPT

British forced back again, 1st to Tobruk Jan/Feb 1942

Tobruk Sidi Barrani

LIBYA El Alamein

El Agheila **Into Egypt May/July 1942**

0   200   EGYPT

THE DESERT WAR

Britain stood alone in 1940, but apart from the struggle on the seas and in the air, only in Africa did the British continue the fight against the Axis on land. Ethiopia was quickly overrun by Wavell's forces, but when British victories in the Western Desert boosted morale at home in 1940–41, Erwin Rommel was sent by Hitler to prop up the Italian forces. Then began the epic struggle between the British Eighth Army and the Afrika Korps.

From the moment that Italy entered the European conflict in 1940, the Desert War was inevitable. Italy had colonial possessions in Africa – Libya, Italian Somaliland, Eritrea, (acquired before World War One) and latterly Ethiopia, seized from Emperor Haile Selassie in 1936. Britain set out to overrun these African territories. After initial reverses, when the Italians took over weakly defended British and French Somaliland, the British bounced back, and as a result of the expert leadership of General Wavell and the fighting skill of Colonel Orde Wingate, the Italians were on the run by 1941. Their entire Nilotic empire was in British hands before the end of that year.

The struggle over Libya, however, was by no means so simple. Once France fell, the Vichy government took effective control over the French colonies of Morocco, Algeria and Tunisia. This gave Italy security in the rear and an opportunity to strike at the lifeline of the British Empire – Egypt and Suez. Despite the British anxieties of

---

Top left: A German 88 fires off a salvo against the Eighth Army. Top right: *Hitler congratulates Rommel upon his promotion.* Left: *Americans land equipment in Algeria after the success of Operation Torch.* Below: *Lieutenant General Dwight D. Eisenhower.*

1940, the Italians won no easy victories. By early 1941 they were in full flight, as the Australians seized Tobruk in January and Benghazi in February. When Cyrenaica fell into British hands and Tripoli was threatened, Hitler decided to send Erwin Rommel to Africa to support his Italian ally, as he had been forced to do in the Balkans. Greece and Crete were being strengthened by British forces just at the moment when Germany was intervening in the African war. This ill-conceived gesture gave Rommel his first opportunity to make progress against weakened British forces in North Africa, which opened the second and most deadly stage in the Desert War: the German advance with the new Afrika Korps.

Rommel's combined Italo-German force pushed to the east, threatening Tobruk, and then besieging the town. After months of spirited defence Tobruk still held, tying up one German and four Italian divisions, but costing the British and Australians all they had gained in 1940. Luck was on the British side as well, for if Rommel had come into the Desert War a few months earlier he might have taken Egypt and Suez. The difference lay in the fact that too many Italian divisions had already been lost to General Sir Richard O'Connor in 1940, and the Axis simply did not have enough time to move more quickly and decisively.

The Middle East looked dangerous for Britain in 1941. Iraq wavered as German infiltration there seemed imminent. Britain, with de Gaulle's blessing, occupied Syria and Lebanon on behalf of the Free French, and Anglo-Russia forces occupied Persia (Iran), blocking a possible German encirclement of the Middle East. But General Wavell had not stopped the Afrika Korps. Churchill replaced him with General Sir Claude Auchinleck, and the newly formed Eighth Army was given to Lt. General Sir Alan Cunningham, whose divisions included many Commonwealth troops from Australia, New Zealand, South Africa and India. Rommel outnumbered him, but was not as strong as he seemed, for the majority of his troops were Italian. By the end of 1941 Tobruk had been relieved, and the Axis was in retreat out of Cyrenaica.

As British forces built up during the lull in the fighting, Rommel decided to take the offensive on 26 May, 1942. He hammered the Free French at Bir Hakeim in the south and forced the British to withdraw from Gazala in the north, exposing Tobruk to German siege once again. A greatly strengthened Afrika Korps, backed up by Stukas, Me 109s and more German armour, assaulted Tobruk and took it on 21 June. This was Germany's first great victory in 1942 and, after the serious setbacks in Russia, it came as a moral

tonic to the Nazis, who were determined to follow up their victory quickly with an invasion of Egypt. Rommel was promoted to Field Marshal and, as Egypt was invaded, something approaching panic gripped the British HQ in Alexandria, where important papers were burned in case the Germans broke through. The British decided to make a stand at El Alamein, flanked by the sea and the impenetrable Qattara Depression – an ocean of sand. Auchinleck was replaced as Commander-in-Chief by General Harold Alexander, and Bernard Montgomery was placed in charge of the Eighth Army.

Rommel was having his difficulties too, mainly supply problems. Because of British naval superiority in the Mediterranean, only about a quarter of the supplies sent to him by sea were arriving, causing him to rely heavily on airlifts. Meanwhile shipments of American Sherman tanks and B-17 bombers (Flying Fortresses) were arriving in Egypt to bolster the Eighth Army. By the end of August Rommel, the 'Desert Fox', made his bid to seize Alexandria before Allied forces became too powerful. He failed to break through at Alam Halfa, and lost many precious tanks. By early September, Allied tanks well outnumbered Rommel's (about 1,000 to 500) and the Afrika Korps was similarly outnumbered by two to one in guns and men.

Montgomery waited until the morale of the Eighth Army had been restored, and with assured superiority, struck on 23 October, 1942, while Rommel was ill and on leave in Germany. Montgomery's purpose was to destroy as much German armour as possible, and this he did at El Alamein. Rommel arrived on the third day of the attack to take over from General von Thoma, but by then a great deal of damage had already been done. Hitler gave the usual order not to

Above: *Sherman tank and ambulance at El Alamein, the turning point in the desert campaign.* Above right: *An unusual periscope used by the Afrika Korps.* Below: *The Desert Fox inspects coastal defences near Tobruk.* Below right: *Lieutenant-General (later Field Marshal Sir) Bernard Montgomery, the victor at Alamein. His inspiration stopped the Nazi drive to Alexandria and started the long retreat of the Afrika Korps out of North Africa. He delayed his counter-attack until he achieved absolute superiority in tanks. After Alamein the Germans withdrew.*

retreat, which caused further losses, and when the order was rescinded on 4 November, Rommel had only about 90 tanks left. Though British losses were high, they still had some 800 tanks as Rommel began his retreat. Alamein was the turning point in the Desert War. It was to be retreat all the way for the Afrika Korps, but Rommel's greatness as a military commander lies in the fact that he kept his force intact, thereby engaging hundreds of thousands of Allied soldiers for almost six months more.

Meanwhile a strong Anglo-American landing force was heading for French North Africa. On 8 November, 1942 Operation Torch hit the beaches of Morocco and Algeria, the first active American contribution to the war in the European Theatre of Operations, and a brilliant Allied counter-stroke. Much of French North Africa was taken almost without a shot being

Below: *Sandstorms were a constant hazard to German and British troops alike.*

fired, and the Afrika Korps was surrounded. The Germans reacted by occupying the rest of France, but were unable to capture the remainder of the French Fleet, which scuttled itself at Toulon. On 12 November the Allies entered Tunisia. The Eighth Army recaptured Tobruk on 13 November and Benghazi was taken a week later.

As Montgomery drove into Tripoli the gates began to close on the Desert Fox. Rommel stopped the Americans at the Kasserine Pass and turned to face the Eighth Army at the Mareth Line. It was a daring but vain attempt to save the situation. The Afrika Korps was beaten back at Medenine on 6 March. The Germans, now without Rommel, who was invalided home, fell back, and held out around Tunis until the Allies closed in. On 12 May came the end in Africa. A quarter of a million Germans and Italians passed into Allied captivity. The first major victory of the war had been gained by the Allies at Alamein. The first victorious Allied campaign had now been won in the Western Desert.

Nevertheless, the Desert War can be seen as an impressive sideshow in World War Two. Hitler could not be defeated in Africa. He had to be beaten in Europe. Most of his troops were committed to the life and death struggle on the Eastern Front. But the loss of so many troops at this crucial moment in the war hurt the Nazis. Italy was now open to invasion. In strategic terms, the fall of North Africa forced Hitler to dispose troops, first to a losing struggle in the desert, then to the support of Mussolini in Italy, at the very moment when he was fighting for his life in Russia. If Alamein was a great moral victory for the Allies, Stalingrad was to prove to be a substantial defeat for Germany. The beginning of the end was near.

Above: *A British tank destroyed near Alamein is inspected by German troops.* Below: *F-4 Wildcat aboard the USS* Ranger *during the landings in North Africa in Operation Torch.*

Far left: *General Erwin Rommel, who was promoted to Field Marshal during the Desert War. He succeeded in tying down the biggest British armed force for two years until he had to retreat to Tunisia.* Left centre: *German tanks are off-loaded in North Africa.* Left: *An Italian merchant ship damaged at Casablanca harbour after the successful landings of Operation Torch in November 1942.* Centre left: *German transport planes continued to ship goods and equipment across the Mediterranean after Britain had secured control of the vital sea lanes.* Centre right: *German motorcyclists in the desert of North Africa.*

Above: *Advancing through the grain fields of the Ukraine. By mid-1942 most of this agricultural heartland of Russia was in German hands.* Above centre: *German infantrymen closely follow their Mark IV tank during the spring offensive of 1943.*

STALINGRAD

Although the Wehrmacht had been stalled before Leningrad and Moscow, it moved forward in the Ukraine until the Russians decided to stand firm before Stalingrad.

By early 1942 Russia had already lost four and a half million men. She had stopped the German offensive, but her back was to the wall. Although many industrial areas were in German hands, her factories had been systematically moved east of the Urals, where most of the country's non-ferrous metals, coal and oil are located. Although many people in western Russia, particularly in the Ukraine, had welcomed the invaders as liberators, their enthusiasm was short-lived as the Germans revealed an increasingly heartless policy towards their new subjects. Dozens of towns were destroyed as reprisals for partisan activities, and the SS began to deport millions of Jews as well as Slavs to extermination camps. The lucky ones spent the war as slave labourers. Eventually the Germans required a quarter of a million troops to police occupied Russia, which further sapped their strength on the front. But the degree to which the subject peoples were prepared to co-operate even with their conquerors is indicated by the fact that between half a million and a million Russians became *Osttruppen* – working in the pay of Germany. The Russian National Liberation Army, later the SS Division Kaminsky, participated in the Warsaw atrocities of 1944, and Kaminsky behaved so terribly that the SS finally killed him. General A. A. Vlasov led an army of 50,000 Russians against the USSR. It was a hard choice between Stalin and Hitler.

Had Hitler treated Russians and Ukrainians as human beings, the war might have ended quite differently. As it was, Germany faced growing partisan activity behind the front from 1942 onwards, which threatened her tenuous supply lines during the crucial years 1942–43.

Hitler had not accepted the fact that failure to achieve victory in 1941 in Russia meant ultimate defeat. In July 1942 he moved his HQ to Vinnitsa in the Ukraine in order to supervise his plan to seize Leningrad and Stalingrad, clear the Crimean peninsula, and occupy the Caucasus up to the Turkish frontier. The Crimea was taken by May 1942 except for Sebastopol, which held out until July, after a 250-day siege reminiscent of its previous ordeal in the Crimean War. Unable to capture Leningrad, the Germans switched emphasis to the south. Two army groups headed for Stalingrad and the Caucasus respectively, but the large gap opening between them was bound to be spotted by the Russians. The Luftwaffe, although outnumbered about three to one, still retained air superiority. Stalin urged his men to dig in. Army Group A could not reach the Caucasus oilfields, and was forced to retreat. Army Group B swept across the Don and advanced to the Volga in August, but the Russians held out at Stalingrad, a key river and rail link. Zhukov was given full powers to defend the city at all costs, but it was General V.I. Chuikov's 62nd Army which

Above right: *A German corporal plants mines during the defence of Stalingrad.* Below: *Joseph Stalin with his Commissar for War Voroshilov. After the purges of the 1930s Stalin surrounded himself with sycophants. His power was unchallenged.*

had the task of actually holding Stalingrad. The German Sixth Army under General Friedrich von Paulus occupied seven-eighths of the city on two occasions – in October and again in November – but Russian artillery across the river was never taken and the Germans were unable to control the river at every point. The fighting in the city was horrific. Buildings were bombarded into rubble and troops were reduced to eating rats. By 23 November Paulus was trapped, and unable to escape, thanks to Hitler's orders never to withdraw. Meanwhile, the Russians moved into the widening gap between Army Groups A and B. The Rumanian Third and Fourth Armies sent to bolster the German Sixth were decimated, so that by the end of November the Sixth Army of 220,000 tired and hungry men had to be supplied by air. Goering swore that his planes could get through – the answer Hitler wanted. His generals implored him to withdraw, but he insisted on standing firm. The Luftwaffe, hampered by the dwindling German perimeter and by fog and

Top left: *Hoth's relief force came within fifty miles of the Stalingrad pocket, but they were unable to break through. Paulus' 6th Army was left to its fate of annhilation and capture.* Left: *Russian T-34 crosses the Volga as the counter-offensive is launched in 1943.* Below left: *Field Marshal von Paulus of the doomed 6th Army who was captured with the remainder of his force at Stalingrad.* Below: *Russian infantrymen press forward against the trapped 6th Army at Kalatsch.* Right: *Stalingrad became the Carthage of the 20th century. The swastika flies in triumph over Red Square in the ruined city. The hammer and sickle soon replaced it.*

cold, could not maintain even a minimal airlift to keep the Sixth Army alive.

Hitler then decided to send in an army group commanded by Field Marshal Erich von Manstein to break the ring around Stalingrad. It had advanced to within 40 miles of the enclave by mid-December; but the Russians prevented the relief of the city. The Sixth Army, as a result of Hitler's obduracy, was doomed. Over 70,000 Germans died in the siege and more than 16,000 were taken prisoner during the fighting. Some gave themselves up after weeks of fatigue, intense combat and short rations. Others committed suicide rather than live a day longer in the hell of Stalingrad. Even dogs drowned themselves in the Volga in preference to enduring the inferno. On 2 February, 1943 it was over. Paulus and 91,000 survivors surrendered, most of them never to return from the rigours of Stalin's prisoner of war camps.

The loss of Stalingrad was a mortal wound to the Third Reich. Hitler's health perceptibly began to fail. He began to take drugs. Stalingrad was too public a defeat even for Dr Goebbels to try to cover up. The reputed invincibility of Nazi troops was a broken myth. Russian pilots had gained the experience and confidence they needed. The Tiger and Panther tanks had met their match in the T–34s and T–70s. From this point on Russian tank production far outstripped Germany's, and their machines were better. Despite the fact that in early 1943 Hitler ruled over more territory than ever before, even he realized that his days were numbered. Stalingrad was the turning point in the war, the beginning of the long German retreat. After this all roads led to Berlin.

Left: *Task Force 16 as seen from the flight deck of the USS* Enterprise *in the Coral Sea.* Top: *The Japanese aircraft carrier* Shoho *under attack during the action.* Above: *A Japanese bomber is shot down on 8 May 1942 during the Battle of the Coral Sea, which was a tactical stalemate but a strategic victory for the US. The Japanese advance toward Australia, which had gone unchecked for the first six months of the war in the Pacific, had finally been stopped.* Below: *The USS* Lexington *blowing up on 8 May 1942 during the Battle of the Coral Sea.*

CORAL SEA AND MIDWAY

The first six months of the war in the Pacific were a tale of defeat and humiliation for the Allies. The bastions of Western imperialism – Hong Kong, Singapore, Manila, Rangoon, Batavia – fell to the Japanese who had also overrun South-East Asia. Turning to Australia and Hawaii they met the remains of the US fleet. The victories of the Coral Sea and Midway were the first in a series of successes for America in the Pacific.

If 1942 was the *annus mirabilis* for the Allies in the Western Desert and at Stalingrad, it was also the year when the war in the Pacific changed course. The incredible speed with which the Japanese swept through South-East Asia encouraged them to believe that conquest would be easy. Their plan was to take the Solomons, wipe out the rest of the American fleet in the Coral Sea, and then move their main fleet eastward to take Midway, Hawaii and the Aleutians, as a preliminary step to an invasion of the US West Coast. The Americans based their naval defence of the Coral Sea on two aircraft carriers, the *Lexington* and *Yorktown*. The Japanese also had two carriers, *Zuikaku* and *Shokaku*. It was the first time in the history of warfare that air power was to decide a naval battle, setting the pattern for many more clashes in the Pacific. The two rival navies never sighted each other, as planes searched the seas for the vital carriers. The battle of the Coral Sea, fought on 6–8 May, 1942, demonstrated that Japan was not invincible. Although the *Lexington* was sunk and the *Yorktown* badly damaged, both Japanese carriers were crippled and put out of action for months. The quality of Japanese pilots, shown so brilliantly at Pearl Harbor, did not run consistently throughout their air corps. They were unused to night operations; their tactics were poor and all their losses heavy. The loss of the few good pilots Japan had were costly, as their replacements were insufficiently trained. And the fact that Japan had been checked in the Coral Sea just after the news

of the fall of Corregidor reached America was a morale-booster at a time when everything seemed to be going badly for the Allies.

Admiral Isoroku Yamamoto, Commander-in-Chief of the Japanese fleet, came to the view that acquisition of further territory was essentially meaningless. Far more important was the destruction of the rest of the US fleet before American industry, now well into war production, replaced the losses. Yamamoto knew that Japan was incapable of fighting a long war, and although not very hopeful of a quick victory, saw Japan's only chance was to eliminate American fighting power from the Pacific in order to persuade the US to sign a negotiated peace. The order therefore went out on 5 May to take Midway Island and the western Aleutians as soon as possible. Midway, with its major airfield, would be useful for raids on the Hawaiian Islands: Adak, Attu and Kiska would give Japan territory in North America and would be a crippling psychological blow to the US if the fleet were engaged by Japan and sunk.

Facing the greatest naval assault force Japan

Above: *The burning hulk of the Mikuma. Above right: Dive bombing of a Japanese carrier at Midway. All four carriers were sunk, and Admiral Yamamoto already knew that the war was lost for Japan. Far right top: Dauntless dive bombers of the US Navy over the smoking wreck of the Japanese cruiser* Mikuma *in the Battle of Midway, 6 June 1942. Bottom left: The* Mogami *capsizing during the Battle of Midway. Bottom right: The US Navy stopped the Japanese advance in the Pacific at Midway. If Midway had been lost, Hawaii and the West Coast of the United States would have been open to attack. After the battle was won the campaign of island-hopping, which led to the four home islands of Japan, began. Centre: The only TBF to get back to Midway on 6 June 1942.*

was ever to amass were Admiral Chester W. Nimitz's 76 ships, including three carriers, *Yorktown, Enterprise* and *Hornet. Yorktown,* which Yamamoto believed had sunk, was made battle-ready in three days rather than weeks or months. Midway itself had a major airfield, giving the Americans four aircraft carriers – the three at sea plus Midway. Against them was a Japanese armada of 162 ships including four carriers and seven battleships in Yamamoto's main strike force. The Americans, however, had two advantages. They had broken the Japanese code so that they knew when and where the Japanese planned to attack. They also had radar, which the Japanese lacked. So when the first Japanese strike force bombed Dutch Harbor in the Aleutians on 3 June and occupied Attu and Kiska on 7 June, the Americans knew it was a feint. When the Japanese sent off 108 planes to attack Midway on the morning of 4 June, radar picked them up 93 miles away. Vice-Admiral Chuichi Nagumo got the shock of his life when American planes, instead of intercepting the Zeros and Zekes, launched attacks on his own carriers. The aircraft were operating from *Enterprise, Hornet* and

Yorktown which, according to Japanese intelligence, simply could not be there. At the end of the day Japan had lost all four of her carriers and 322 aircraft. The US lost 150 planes and the *Yorktown.*

The victory was complete. The Japanese bid for supremacy in the Pacific had failed. As they limped away from the scene on 6 June they realized that, despite Pearl Harbor and all their conquests, they were in desperate straits. It was likely to be a long war, in which case they would lose. As Nimitz said, 'Pearl Harbor has been partially avenged.' Midway was the turning point in the Pacific War. The road to Hiroshima, and to the humiliation of Japan was now open.

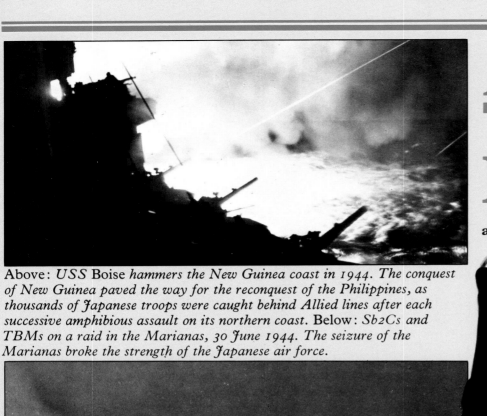

Above: *USS* Boise *hammers the New Guinea coast in 1944. The conquest of New Guinea paved the way for the reconquest of the Philippines, as thousands of Japanese troops were caught behind Allied lines after each successive amphibious assault on its northern coast. Below: Sb2Cs and TBMs on a raid in the Marianas, 30 June 1944. The seizure of the Marianas broke the strength of the Japanese air force.*

ACROSS THE PACIFIC

There was only one way to get to Japan: across the Pacific to the home islands by encircling the chain of island fortresses which barred the path of the Allies. But at certain points the Japanese had to be attacked head-on: New Guinea and Guadalcanal.

Since March 1942 there had been a divided American command in the Pacific War. Admiral Nimitz was in charge of the essentially naval war, island-hopping across the Pacific toward the four home islands of Japan. General MacArthur controlled operations in Australia, New Guinea, the Solomons, most of the Dutch East Indies, and the Philippines (to which he had promised to return). Since every landing in the Pacific was a combined operation, the division of authority can only be seen in the context of US intra-service rivalry in general and of MacArthur's personality in particular. MacArthur was not a man who liked taking orders from anyone. Impatient with Roosevelt for having put Europe first in the line of priority, and jealous of other service commanders, he ran his own show from the outset, struggling with equal vigour against the Joint Chiefs of Staff and the Japanese. But partly as a result of MacArthur's pressure and partly because of the initial hatred and anger engendered in America by Pearl Harbor, roughly twice the amount of equipment went to the Pacific, where the threat to the United States was more immediate, than to the European Theatre of Operations during the first months following the American involvement. After Midway, however, the emphasis shifted to Europe until well into 1944. Whereas victory over Japan seemed only a matter of means and time, in 1943 the tide could still have turned either way in the war with Hitler.

It was the navy which was given first crack at pushing back the Japanese wave from an island in the Solomons near Australia, previously unknown to the world, but whose very name spells US Marine Corps – Guadalcanal.

The airstrip on Guadalcanal was necessary for

Top left: *Four riflemen of an advance patrol seek out the enemy. These Americans won the Distinguished Service Cross for their efforts on 21 January 1943.* Top right: *Marines scramble up the beach at Tarawa in November 1943.* Above: *A marine with fixed bayonet prepares to advance on Eniwetok atoll in February 1944.* Left: *A damaged Japanese ship near Cape Esperance, Guadalcanal, in the Solomons. The seizure of Guadalcanal was a tough time for the US Marines, who took the island in 1943 after suffering severe casualties.*

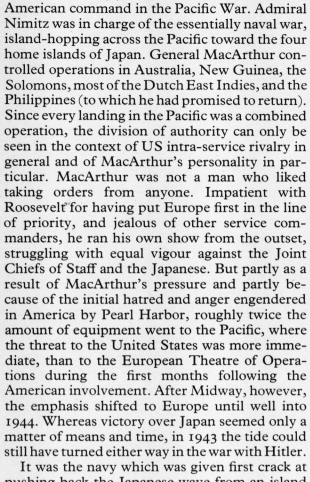

Above: *Members of the 503rd Parachute Infantry land at Kamiri airstrip on Noemfoor Island in Dutch New Guinea, 2 July, 1944.* Above centre: *Marines await the word to advance as they are pinned down by enemy fire on the beach at Peleliu.*

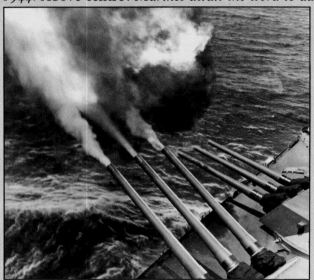

Above: *USS* Iowa *bombards Tinian in mid-July 1944 prior to the landing.* Above centre: *US Marines advance into the interior of Guam, July 1944.* Above right: *Amphibious tank and men of the 6th Cavalry Reconnaissance Company in the jungle of Dutch New Guinea, August 1944.*

the protection of Australia, and the full meaning of jungle warfare was made plain to the Marines who fought for six months to take the island. Bombarded from the sea, the US Navy was forced to engage the Japanese fleet six times. Each side lost 24 ships, at a time when the Americans could least afford the sacrifice. Above all, the slaughter of Guadalcanal and the difficulty in taking it (the fighting lasted over six months, from August 1942 to February 1943) convinced the US that to fight inch by inch across the Pacific would be as suicidal as it would be tedious. A better method had to be found.

MacArthur initiated the new strategy in New Guinea. Instead of pushing the Japanese back along the coasts and through the jungle, he bypassed enemy forces by means of several amphibious invasions along the north coast, behind their lines, achieving his aim by encirclement instead of frontal assault. Gona and Buna on New Guinea were lost to Japan; Lae was fortified and subsequently lost. The Americans pushed relentlessly westward across the north coast of New Guinea. The death of Yamamoto, whose plane was shot down by the Americans in April 1943, was an additional bonus. But the Allied gains in 1943 in the Pacific were not impressive until the end of the year, when Rabaul on New Britain was hit so hard by US planes that the Japanese air force was withdrawn to the island of Truk. By the end of the year Americans had landed on New Britain. Rabaul was encircled, its 100,000 defenders surrounded by sea controlled by the Allies. Pressure on Australia was relieved, and the Japanese were on the defensive in the Solomons and New Guinea.

Meanwhile, Nimitz's drive toward Japan was gathering momentum. What was required was a series of air bases close enough to strike at Japanese cities and industrial targets with the big bombers now being developed – the B-29 Superfortresses, more powerful versions of the Flying Fortresses which had become a mainstay of the Allied bombing missions over Germany in 1943. After a brutal struggle to take Tarawa in the Gilbert Islands at the end of 1943 and the quick clearance of the Marshall Islands in early 1944, Turk, in the Carolines became the next objective. As the Japanese perimeter of defence in the Pacific narrowed, the fighting of their soldiers became more fanatically stubborn. On each island they had to be rooted out from foxholes, bunkers and trees. Often they fought to the last man. Surrender meant dishonour to the soldiers who had sworn to uphold the feudal warrior code of Bushido. The Marines, who usually made the landings, resorted to every weapon in their armoury – hand grenades, TNT, flame throwers and machine guns, as well as straight hand-to-hand fighting. Naval bombardment and increasing air superiority made the landings less difficult, but there was no alternative to rooting out every single Japanese soldier from the Pacific islands. By mid-1944 the Americans had broken into the most powerful group of islands in the Japanese defence line – the Marianas. The two-pronged offensive was working. Nimitz and MacArthur were pressing toward the Philippines. The Americans were closer to their goal of capturing the strategic bases in the Pacific which would make saturation bombing of Japan possible.

Top right: *Admirals Nimitz and Spruance, architects of the victory of the Philippine Sea, which paved the way for the destruction of the remainder of the Japanese fleet at Leyte Gulf.* Below: *Marines keep their rifles dry as they move toward the beach of Tinian in August 1944.*

ITALY-THE HARD UNDERBELLY

Churchill described the Mediterranean flank of the Axis as the 'soft underbelly' of Fortress Europe. When the Allies attacked Sicily and Italy, they found it anything but soft. It took two years to wrest the long peninsula from Hitler's iron grip.

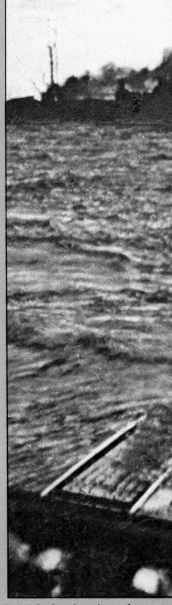

The end in Africa was quickly followed by the next logical step – the invasion of Italy. The Germans were expecting an attack in the Mediterranean to follow the fall of Tunisia, but they were uncertain where the invasion would take place. Greece was suggested; Sardinia was considered more likely. In the event the chosen target was the island of Sicily, the decision to invade being taken by Roosevelt and Churchill at the Casablanca Conference in January 1943. Mussolini could not count on the loyalty of Sicilians. After having taken power in 1922 he had gradually weakened the hold of the Mafia on the island; not surprisingly its members in America found it convenient to declare their patriotism to the US when they saw the prospect of Mussolini's departure. But no decision had been reached at Casablanca about the next step. Churchill felt that the Mediterranean was Europe's 'soft underbelly' and that an attack in this area would hurt Hitler where he was weakest. At the same time, it would give the British and Americans a chance to move into Greece, Yugoslavia and Italy, thereby strengthening the southern flank of Europe against the inevitable spread of Communism which would accompany an Allied, and therefore Russian victory. Churchill also argued that the liberation of France could be more easily facilitated by landings in Italy. Roosevelt was far less convinced that this was the right step; and Stalin was certainly opposed. He had pressed the Allies for a year and a half to open a second front in Europe to relieve the pressure on Stalingrad, Moscow and Leningrad. Operation Torch appeased him temporarily, but he made it plain later to FDR and Churchill at the Teheran Conference in late November 1943 that he intended to establish a cordon of friendly states in Eastern Europe after the war. The 'soft underbelly' approach would be an effective counter-move towards postwar control of the Balkans, as Churchill well knew. But Roosevelt's chief concern was with winning the war, and he tended to agree with 'Uncle Joe' Stalin that Germany could not be defeated by an attack on Italy. It would have to be through France, aiming at the industrial heartland of Germany – the Ruhr.

In the event, however, a modified version of Churchill's plan was adopted. Sicily would be secured, and the Allies would then fight their way up the 'boot' of Italy. Italian troops would have to be withdrawn from the Eastern Front (pleasing Stalin) and bombing raids on south Germany could be launched from Italian air-

Below: Members of the 143rd Infantry Regiment Combat Team on the Salerno beaches. Above centre: British domination of the central Mediterranean was crucial to the success of an Allied advance in Italy. After the Battle of Matapan in 1941 the British only had to fear the occasional U-boat.

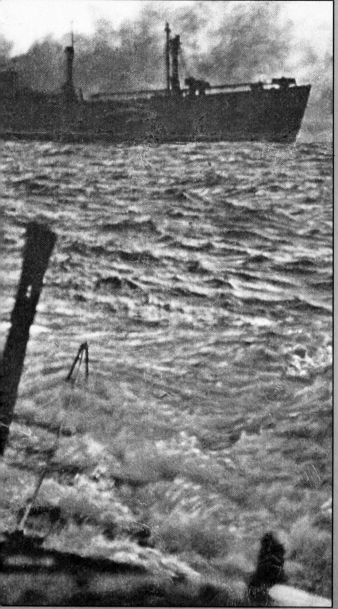

Allied troops landing by sea

22.7.43

Allied advance and dates
of capture

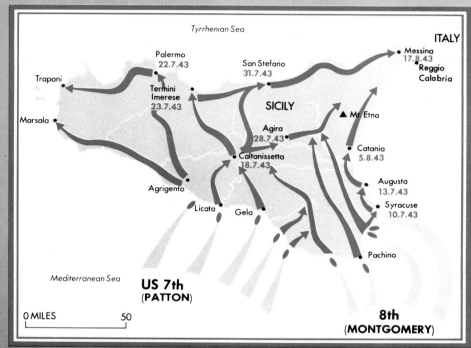

Tyrrhenian Sea

ITALY

Palermo
22.7.43

San Stefano
31.7.43

Messina
17.8.43

Reggio
Calabria

Trapani

Termini
Imerese
23.7.43

SICILY

▲ Mt. Etna

Marsala

Agira
28.7.43

Catania
5.8.43

Caltanissetta
18.7.43

Agrigento

Augusta
13.7.43

Licata

Gela

Syracuse
10.7.43

Pachino

Mediterranean Sea

US 7th
(PATTON)

0 MILES   50

8th
(MONTGOMERY)

Top right: *The British cruiser* Orion *advances during the bombardment of Pantelleria, 11 June 1943. The easy capture of this undefended island was soon followed by the next step in the Italian campaign, the capture of Sicily.*

fields. Moreover, one of Hitler's allies could be toppled. All depended on the speed and efficacy of the Sicilian campaign. The Allied landings on 10 July, 1943 were almost unopposed, despite the fact that there were about 230,000 Italian and some 40,000 German troops on the island. The British Eighth Army under Montgomery struck at the right flank, while General George Patton's American Third Army attacked the left. The first wave of the invasion brought 160,000 Allied soldiers to Sicily and 600 tanks, backed by a fleet of 750 vessels and 4,000 aircraft. Victory was swift. Within a month the island was conquered, the Americans arriving at Messina just before the British. Full co-operation was given to the Allies by the civilian population, partially with the help of the Mafia, which re-established effective control of the villages.

The conquest of Sicily marked the end of Italy's role as an Axis partner. On 25 July King Victor Emmanuel III appointed Marshal Pietro Badoglio, the hero of Ethiopia, to replace Mussolini who was immediately imprisoned. But it was not the end of German control over Italy. Although the Italian Fleet soon passed into Allied hands, and Badoglio signed an armistice with the Allies on 3 September – the day the Allies made their first landing in Italy at Reggio Calabria – the Germans moved quickly to seize Rome and all the major airfields. The King and his government fled to Brindisi, and on 9 September General Mark Clark's Fifth Army landed in the Gulf of Salerno. The port of Taranto was captured by the British on the same day. Three days later Mussolini was kidnapped by an officer of the SS, Otto Skorzeny, in a daring surprise raid. Il Duce was flown to Germany and later installed in a puppet regime in Salo in the far north of the country, which achieved little popular support. It was Hitler's justification for remaining in Italy.

On 13 October the Italian government declared

Top left: *Marshal Pietro Badoglio, who took over the Italian state and prepared the terms of surrender to the Allies after Mussolini was toppled.*
Above: *An Me-109 strafes a US landing party on the Salerno beach-head.*
Below: *Bazookas are fired into a house by infantrymen of the US Fifth Army near Anzio, after a successful amphibious landing on the Italian coast.* Opposite top: *Softening up the beach at Anzio prior to the Allied landing.*

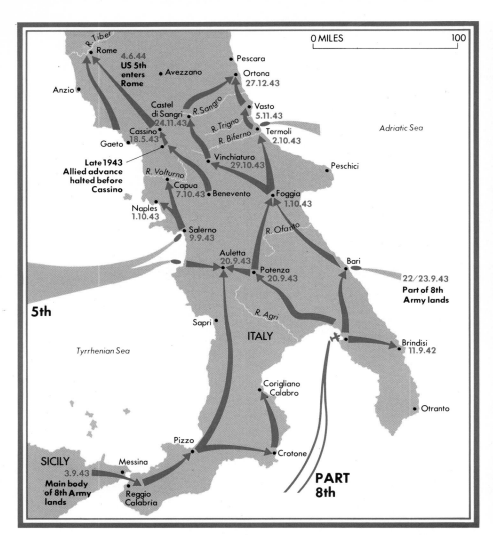

Map labels:

R. Tiber
Rome
4.6.44
US 5th enters Rome
Anzio
Pescara
Avezzano
Ortona 27.12.43
Castel di Sangri 24.11.43
R. Sangro
Vasto 5.11.43
Cassino 18.5.43
R. Trigno
Gaeto
R. Biferno
Termoli 2.10.43
Adriatic Sea
Late 1943 Allied advance halted before Cassino
Vinchiaturo 29.10.43
R. Volturno
Capua 7.10.43
Benevento
Foggia 1.10.43
Peschici
Naples 1.10.43
Salerno 9.9.43
R. Ofanto
5th
Auletta 20.9.43
Bari
Potenza 20.9.43
22/23.9.43 Part of 8th Army lands
Sapri
R. Agri
ITALY
Tyrrhenian Sea
Brindisi 11.9.42
Corigliano Calabro
Otranto
Pizzo
SICILY
3.9.43
Messina
Crotone
PART 8th
Main body of 8th Army lands
Reggio Calabria

0 MILES   100

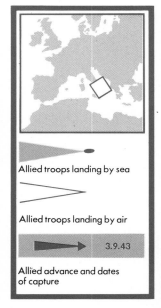

Legend:
Allied troops landing by sea
Allied troops landing by air
3.9.43
Allied advance and dates of capture

Right: *Field Marshal von Kesselring and an Italian general inspect troops. Kesselring masterminded the German resistance in Italy, which tied up thousands of Allied troops who might have been sent to France.*
Far right: *Generals Alexander, Clark and McCreedy inspect the Anzio beach.*

war on Germany, with the Allies now in effective occupation of the south of the country. For most Italians the last stages of the war were particularly difficult. Many anti-Fascists made their way south to join Badoglio or the Allied armies, but for others it was a choice between resistance and sullen silence. Field Marshal Albert von Kesselring, in charge of German operations in Italy, suppressed the Communists and less radical patriotic groups who welcomed the invasion and set up a line of defence south of Rome – the Gustav Line – which the Allies attempted to break.

The build up of Allied forces in Britain in preparation for Operation Overlord – the invasion of France – hindered Allied progress in Italy. General Dwight D. Eisenhower (since Operation Torch in charge of American operations) went to England in December, together with General Montgomery, Lt. General Omar Bradley and Air Chief Marshal Sir Arthur Tedder, head of British air operations. Eisenhower's Italian command was taken by General Sir Henry Maitland-Wilson, and Lt. General Sir Oliver Leese took over the British Eighth Army. Mark Clark was left as the senior American in charge of the Fifth Army. The Allies had twenty divisions under Clark and Alexander, while Kesselring had eighteen, eight of which were

Left: *Machine gunners of a patrol only 400 yards from enemy lines at the Anzio beach-head fire from the cover of an abandoned house.*

kept in reserve or to hold down northern Italy; so the Germans were operationally outnumbered by a ratio of two to one.

The Battle of the Garigliano began in mid-January 1944. Major-General Lucas landed some 50,000 Allies on the beaches of Anzio on 22 January north of the Gustav Line, and was pinned down by German forces who contained the beachhead. On the Garigliano the Germans stood firm, using the fortress–abbey of Monte Cassino as an observation post and barrier to the Allied drive north. Having hesitated because of the historical importance and beauty of Monte Cassino, the Allies received permission from the Pope to attack and destroy it once it became clear that the Germans were fortifying it and planned to defend it to the end. On 15 February the abbey was bombed into rubble. It did not fall, despite subsequent attacks on the mountain. On 15 March a second aerial assault was followed by an artillery bombardment. The subsequent attack with tanks and infantry was halted after eight days of fruitless blood-letting. The fortress was finally taken after the Allies had broken the Gustav Line and the Germans had been out-flanked. The capture of Monte Cassino on 17 May and the surrender of Rome on 4 June marked the end of the major offensive in Italy. Operation Overlord was to take far greater precedence in the following months. The Allied armies in Italy were constantly weakened by the removal of troops to France later in 1944. But the cost to Germany was tremendous. Just at the moment when the Anglo-Americans were plunging into Western Europe and the Russians were moving into Poland, the Germans were obliged to weaken their other fronts by sending 25 divisions into Italy.

Kesselring retreated to the Gothic Line north of Florence, which was taken on 4 August. But the swift advance up the peninsula was halted by the autumn. The Allied intervention was to keep Germany occupied while more important advances were made elsewhere; and as the Allied armies were milked, Hitler withdrew some of his troops to protect the Reich. It was not until the early spring of 1945 that the final chapter of the Italian campaign would be written.

Above right: *The ruins of the famous Abbey after its capture. What remained looked like a series of caves in the hillside.* Right: *Mussolini, after his capture by Otto Skorzeny. Il Duce was forced to return to Italy to lead the puppet Salo Republic during the last year and a half of the war, which gave Hitler the thin pretext he required to keep his forces in Italy and delay the Allied advance northward.* Far right: *The bombardment of Monte Cassino, which was permitted by Pope Pius XII after consultation with the Allied command. It was used as a fortress blocking the Allied march northward.*

KURSK & THE RUSSIAN COUNTER-OFFENSIVE

The setback the German Sixth Army suffered at Stalingrad was the beginning of the end of Germany's fight for control of Soviet Russia. As the Nazis fell back they regrouped and planned a counter-attack. The Battle of Kursk in the summer of 1943 was the biggest tank battle fought in history. It broke the back of the Third Reich. The Wehrmacht retreated a thousand miles leaving devastation and suffering in its wake.

After the fall of Stalingrad, the Germans paused to regroup and face the inevitable Russian counter-offensive. Some of Germany's allies, notably the Italians, were demoralized, but others, like the Bulgarians and Hungarians, fought well on the front lines. By the end of 1943 some 30 divisions were to be disbanded for want of replacements. But the Germans were still holding their own. Manstein received permission from Hitler to withdraw to the Donets, which enabled the Russians to take Kharkov, but in mid-February 1943 the Germans counter-attacked and by mid-March had retaken the area. The withdrawal had its advantages. The split in the German ranks had been closed, and the passage of time allowed reserves of considerable strength to build up in the German rear. The Allied bombing missions over Germany, which began to intensify at this point, reaching a crescendo in late 1944, had little effect on Nazi war production. Thanks to the work of Albert Speer, who was placed in effective charge of the entire German economic machine, industrial production actually grew during the years when the bombing of German factories and cities turned soft, summer evenings into nights of hell. Hamburg was destroyed in July. Germany was out of Africa. Sicily had been invaded. But German factories were turning out Pzkw IVs at

Below: *Albert Speer, by 1943 in full charge of the German economy, inspects a captured T-34 tank. Speer, Hitler's architect in prewar days, galvanized the war machine into production for total war, so that, despite saturation bombing of Germany by the Allies, industrial production actually increased considerably in 1943–44.*
Below centre: *General Nikolai Vatutin, hero of the Battle of Kursk, where German forces made their final attempt to master the Soviet Union.*

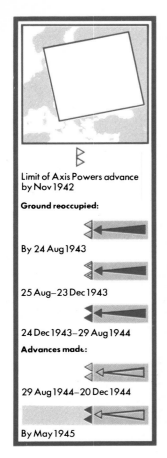

Limit of Axis Powers advance
by Nov 1942

Ground reoccupied:

By 24 Aug 1943

25 Aug–23 Dec 1943

24 Dec 1943–29 Aug 1944

Advances made:

29 Aug 1944–20 Dec 1944

By May 1945

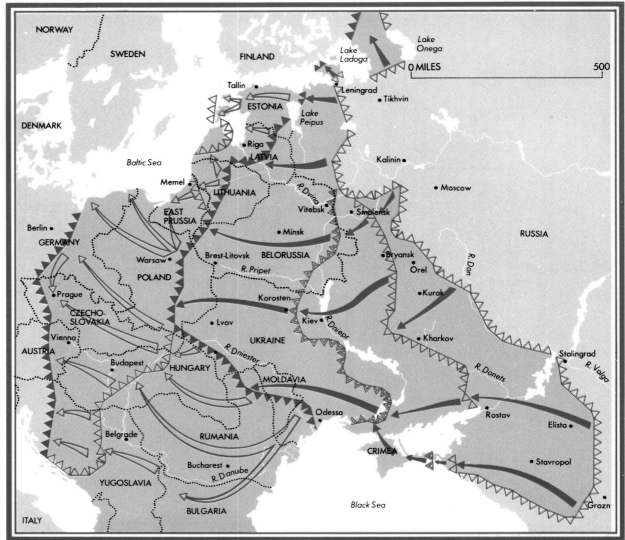

Left: *Marshal I. S. Koniev, commander-in-chief of the offensive in the Ukraine which swept into southern Poland and Silesia in 1944.* Above right: *German Pzkw IVs, Panthers and Tigers sweep forward into the Kursk salient in the summer of 1943.* Below: *Western Russia was devastated twice, first during Operation Barbarossa, and again during the scorched earth retreat to Poland after Kursk.*

the rate of 2,000 a month, and the more advanced Tiger and Panther tanks were also being produced at an increasing rate. Heinz Guderian was recalled to active service to supervise the German military machine. He was convinced (more so than Stalin) that the Allies would attempt a landing in France later in 1943. He implored the Führer to hold the line in the East in order to prepare the Atlantic Wall and build up forces in the West. Hitler, despite the fact that he agreed with Guderian, doggedly refused either to allow withdrawals in the East or to cancel his plans for a summer offensive. Hold the line everywhere was his policy; attack in the East was his goal.

After Stalingrad, Russian advances south of Orel and north of Kharkov, (both of which were in German hands) had won them control of Kursk. Hitler planned to attack this Kursk salient, and the massive offensive was launched on 5 July with almost one million men and 2,700 tanks. A double envelopment was planned with Kluge and Model striking from the north and Manstein and Hoth advancing from the south. But Zhukov expected such a manoeuvre. He had more tanks (3,600), and his one and a quarter million troops were prepared and well-equipped. The Russians held the German thrust from the

north effectively, but Hoth made good initial progress. General Nikolai Vatutin was thrown back, and General Ivan Koniev's reserves were brought up to fight the biggest tank battle in the war on 12 July. The German Tigers, without machine guns or light tanks to support them, were easy targets. The T-34s and heavier Russian tanks proved to be more than equal to the challenge. By the end of the day the last great German offensive in the East had been stopped. The following morning Hitler cancelled the operation and the great withdrawal took place. Half a million Germans were lost at Kursk and, with them, every German chance of victory. It was to be a long road back.

The Russian advance in the wake of Kursk was swift and decisive. Orel was liberated on 4 August and Kharkov on 23 August. The whole front was pushed back hundreds of miles. The Crimea was being evacuated. The Germans hoped to hold the line at the Dnieper, but in other sectors their front was falling back too. Smolensk was liberated on 25 September, finally relieving the pressure on Moscow. During the retreat the casualty rate was high and there were insufficient replacements. The Russians, who had received considerable economic aid in terms

and Pruth and on into Rumania at the end of March. The Russian offensive, which in eight months had almost cleared the Soviet Union of the Wehrmacht, then paused briefly. Hitler appointed Model to replace the exhausted Manstein as Commander-in-Chief in late March, claiming that the Russian offensive had passed its peak. But with over seven million men under arms, Russia had only just begun its series of victories.

In April the advance in the Crimea began and the Germans were forced back to Sebastopol, which fell in early May. Finland left the war in June, after the Mannerheim Line was broken. On the third anniversary of the launching of Operation Barbarossa, Russia began her greatest drive of all, concentrating 179 divisions under Marshals Zhukov and Vasilevsky to complete her reconquest of the Ukraine, with the aid of 150,000 partisans operating behind German lines. Army Group South virtually collapsed in three weeks, and 350,000 Germans were taken prisoner. In the centre Minsk was surrounded and fell on 3 July. Ten days later the capital of Lithuania, Vilna, was captured. The Russians were advancing at a rate of ten to fifteen miles per day. It was now a month after D-Day, which had taken place on 6 June, and Germany herself was open to invasion from Russia and France. The bomb plot of 20 July almost cost Hitler his life, and led him, at this moment of crisis, to purge his general staff, many of whom were implicated in the assassination attempt, hoping for a negotiated peace with the Allies.

The end seemed to be approaching fast. As Soviet troops entered Poland, German resistance stiffened, for now the prospect loomed of defending the Reich itself. With the Russians in sight of Warsaw, the people of the city rose to attack the Germans on 1 August. Within a week the Poles had almost seized their capital. The RAF tried to drop supplies into the tortured city, but the Russians, admittedly exhausted after their long advance, paused and refused to cross the river between their forces and Warsaw to relieve the Poles. The SS committed some of its most horrible atrocities in Warsaw, impaling babies on bayonets, using flame throwers to root out resistance, and burning prisoners alive. The Poles, without support, fighting from rooftops and sewers, were forced to capitulate on 2 October. About 90 per cent of Warsaw was razed to the ground, and the Germans were able to hold out there until January 1945. The cost of the rising was terrible, some 300,000 Poles losing their lives. Many have criticized the Russians for failing to relieve Warsaw. Actually, their supply lines were over-extended and their troops needed a rest after the long advance. But when they realized that the Nazis were making the way easier for them to establish a Russian-oriented government in Warsaw after the war by wiping out the city, the Russians chose to stay on the east side of the Dnieper and watch the slaughter. The strategic effect of this bloodbath was to halt the Russian drive through the centre. Their offensive concentrated on the south. In August Russian troops pushed through Rumania, forc-

of clothing, trucks and munitions from America, possessed ample reserves in materials and manpower. As the Russian military machine gained momentum, Germany's slowly ran out of steam. The economic war of attrition was finally taking its toll, as the Germans were forced to bolster their defences elsewhere, as in Italy. The crisis was not the result of strategic bombing, (which, despite the unnecessary slaughter of civilians, had little effect on the German war effort) but due to the simple fact that Germany's population and resources were unequal to the task of taking on the combined strength of America, the Soviet Union and the British Empire at the same time.

The Russian Leviathan pushed relentlessly westward. The liberation of Kiev on 6 November breached the Dnieper defence line. By now German soldiers were outnumbered two to one and Russian superiority in tanks and guns was beginning to have its effect. Hitler at last followed Guderian's advice and bolstered his forces in the West. This inevitably meant abandoning his defence line in the East. Leningrad, under siege since 1941, was finally relieved in January 1944, as the Nazis retreated to Estonia. The entire front was beginning to crack. The Russians pushed across the Dniester, Bug

Below: *Admiral Nicholas Horthy, dictator of Hungary, who tried to abandon the alliance with Hitler as Russian soldiers approached his borders. Like Mussolini, he was kidnapped and sent to Germany by Skorzeny. Unlike Il Duce, however, he survived the war and died in modest comfort in Portugal in the 1950s. Below centre: Street fighting in Schtomin during the German retreat. Below right: Backs to the wall: the Wehrmacht's defence of Poland was fierce.*

Below right: *Hitler greets wounded soldiers back from the Russian front in 1943. The manpower pool was dwindling fast, and school children were eventually called up to fight side by side with sexogenarians in the final defence of the Reich.* Bottom: *A downed Russian plane is examined by German technicians. Despite its numerical superiority the Russian air force was never a match for the Luftwaffe – until the closing stages of the war.*

ing that country to surrender. A month later Bulgaria fell and declared war on Germany. In October Admiral Horthy, the Hungarian dictator, abandoned his Nazi ally. He was sent to the Reich as a prisoner and German troops took over the country. In December Budapest was encircled by the Russians. By mid-1944 it was evident that Germany had lost the war in the East and that total defeat was only a matter of time. The effect of the collapse of German power in Eastern Europe was terrible. The transportation of Jews to extermination camps, which had begun in 1941, was stepped up. Nazi atrocities in occupied territories, now abandoned, left a heritage of hatred in their wake. Russian soldiers were often enthusiastically welcomed by civilians,

despite the fact that they raped, looted and pillaged their way into Poland, the Balkans and, finally, Germany. Their crimes equalled those of the retreating Germans, whose lack of discipline caused even Guderian and many Wehrmacht officers to protest. It is hard to compare degrees of inhumanity. Suffice it to say that both the Russians and Germans treated their prisoners bestially; both administered huge slave labour camps; both practised extermination policies on their own and their neighbours' populations. In many ways the war in the East typified World War Two as a whole – an unspeakable accumulation of crimes against civilians and belligerents alike. By mid-1944 Germany had lost the war in the East. Therefore Germany had lost the war.

OVERLORD AND ANVIL

For two years Eisenhower planned the return of the Western Allies to France. Hitler expected the attack, but its timing and location remained a well-kept secret.

As early as May 1943, an invasion of France by Britain and the United States had been planned for the following year, thus opening the second front for which Stalin had long been pleading. Germany was well prepared, and by the summer of 1944 60 divisions were positioned in the West to repel the invasion. In December 1943 General Eisenhower was placed in charge of the Allied expeditionary force, with Air Chief Marshal Tedder as his Deputy Commander. The actual landings were to be made by the American First Army, under the command of Lt. General Omar Bradley, and the British Second Army, under Lt. General Sir Miles Dempsey. They would have at their disposal eight divisions, comprising 150,000 men to be landed within 48 hours of D-Day. The 60 German divisions were spread from the Dutch coast to the Bay of Biscay. The Commander-in-Chief in the West, Field Marshal von Rundstedt, claimed that these forces were over-extended, and Erwin Rommel, recalled in November 1943 to advise Hitler about the efficacy of the Atlantic Wall, reported that this was correct. But their conclusions differed. Rundstedt suggested that if an invasion were to occur, as was probable, the Germans should retreat to the German frontier. Rommel insisted

Above: *Hitler would have preferred the Atlantic Wall to have run from Biarritz to Bremen. Goebbels' Propaganda Ministry pretended that heavy guns like this protected all of Fortress Europe.* Top: *The reality of the Atlantic Wall.*

Above: *Expectancy in every face: part of the D-Day invasion force.* Below: *Americans assault Omaha Beach on D-Day, 6 June 1944. This bungled effort almost ruined Eisenhower's plans for a successful invasion of France.*

Above: Barrage balloons protect the invasion force, which built up to 150,000 men once the landings on the five D-Day beaches had been secured. Below right: *The big guns of the USS* Nevada *soften up the French coast prior to the Normandy landings.*

that if the Allies were to stay on the beaches more than 48 hours, the war would be lost. In February 1944 Rommel was put in charge of the defence of the West, although Rundstedt retained overall command. Both agreed that the invasion would take place at Calais, the narrowest stretch of water between England and France, but Hitler thought that Normandy would be the most likely target. Fortunately for the Allies, Hitler followed the advice of his generals on this occasion.

Rommel had only eighteen divisions available in Normandy. Against these the Allies built up a formidable air superiority; 7,500 fighters were commissioned to protect the landings, which would be supported by over 5,000 naval craft of all types. A squadron of 3,500 bombers ham-

mered French road and rail links, which were also sabotaged by French resistance fighters, the Maquis. At two o'clock in the morning of 6 June, 1944 Allied paratroops began to drop on the areas behind some of the five beaches in Normandy where the main Allied forces were to land. The first objective was to take Caen and cut off the Cotentin peninsula; after that there would be a drive up the Seine Valley to Paris. At Utah Beach the Americans made a highly successful landing, despite some confusion caused by inexperienced paratroops. But on Omaha Beach, the second American landing, casualties were heavy. This landing was totally botched, and the whole operation would have been placed in jeopardy had it not been for the success at Utah

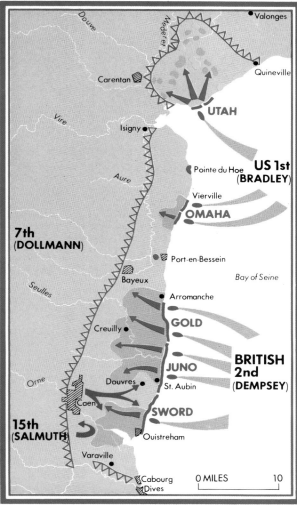

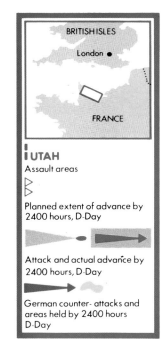

Valonges

Douve

Mederet

Carentan

Quineville

UTAH

Isigny

Vire

US 1st
(BRADLEY)

Aure

Pointe du Hoe

Vierville

OMAHA

7th
(DOLLMANN)

Port-en-Bessein

Bay of Seine

Seulles

Bayeux

Arromanche

GOLD

Creuilly

Orne

Douvres

JUNO

St. Aubin

BRITISH
2nd
(DEMPSEY)

Caen

SWORD

15th
(SALMUTH)

Ouistreham

Varaville

0 MILES   10

Cabourg
Dives

BRITISH ISLES

London

FRANCE

i UTAH
Assault areas

▷ ▷

Planned extent of advance by
2400 hours, D-Day

Attack and actual advance by
2400 hours, D-Day

German counter- attacks and
areas held by 2400 hours
D-Day

*Right: Montgomery greets General de Gaulle on
French soil a week after the invasion of Normandy.*

and on the three British beaches, Gold, Juno and Sword. Rommel, shocked by the landings, returned from home leave in Germany to find the Allies firmly entrenched on the beaches within 48 hours, enabling thousands of troops and tens of thousands of tons of equipment to be landed each day. German forces were hurriedly shifted from the Pas de Calais area, but too late. Nevertheless, local resistance was fierce. Rundstedt was ousted by Hitler on 1 July and replaced by Kluge. Soon afterwards Rommel was put out of action when his car was hit by Allied aircraft. In a desperate effort to turn the tide, Hitler launched his secret V-1 weapons against London. The dreadful 'buzz-bombs' caused considerable damage and civilian casualties but had little effect upon the outcome of the struggle in France.

On 17 August Kluge was replaced as Commander-in-Chief by Model, whose main task was to prevent a breakout from the Normandy beachhead. Two days before his appointment, the Allies began Operation Anvil, the follow-up to Operation Overlord, landing ten divisions near Cannes in southern France. The Germans rapidly evacuated the south as partisans rose in revolt in Paris. Rommel, partially implicated in the 20 July plot to kill Hitler, was forced to commit suicide. Kluge also took his own life after begging Hitler to end the war at once. A week later General Dietrich von Choltitz disobeyed Hitler's orders to destroy Paris and resist to the end when he surrendered the capital intact to the French. On the following day, 26 August, General de Gaulle led a victory parade through the streets of Paris while a few diehard Germans and collaborators sniped at him from the rooftops. By September, the battle for France was virtually over. It had cost Germany half a million casualties, including 210,000 prisoners taken.

France was almost cleared of Germans but Hitler ordered the Wehrmacht to hold the key ports at all costs. Brest was not captured until 18 September, and remaining pockets of resistance temporarily checked a further Allied advance. But in the north the Allies thrust into Belgium, recapturing Brussels on 3 September and Antwerp on the following day. Montgomery hoped to bring the war to a speedy conclusion by sending three airborne divisions into Holland to outflank the Siegfried Line, where German resistance was stiffening. The American parachute landings at Eindhoven and Nijmegen opened the Maas and Waal Rivers to the Allies, but the attempt to clear the Lower Rhine was a failure because the British paratroops landed too far from the bridge at Arnhem to secure the area. A few broke out and returned to their lines, but more than half the force of 10,000 paratroops who landed were captured and over a thousand were killed. The so-called Operation Market-Garden was a disaster. By the end of September the Germans had taken a stand and their lines held. Most of Holland remained in German hands, isolated until the end of the war. With the Russians checked before Warsaw and the Anglo-Americans stalled, Hitler gained time to plan a final counter-attack. His last offensive came in December at the Battle of the Bulge.

Below: *The 'bridge too far' over the Rhine at Arnhem. Most of the British and Allied troops that tried to take it were either killed or captured.*

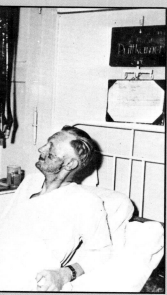

Top left: *Hitler holds his injured right hand after the abortive bomb plot of 20 July 1944. If von Stauffenberg had placed his briefcase carrying the bomb under the right place, Hitler would have been killed and the German generals would have sued for a negotiated peace. The failure of the bomb plot made the Allies' threat of an unconditional surrender a certainty, for Hitler planned to fight on until the bitter end.* Above left: *Hitler visits Puttkamer, who was more seriously injured by the bomb plot than its intended victim.* Top centre: *American infantrymen near St Lo, while the Allies attempt to break out of the Normandy beach-head.* Above centre: *A US soldier races past a knocked out tank destroyer in St Lo. German snipers infested the town and impeded the Allied advance.* Top right: *Allied aircraft over Valkenswaard, south of Eindhoven.* Above right: *Parachutists drop into Holland in the first stages of the ill-fated Operation Market-Garden.*

THE ARDENNES OFFENSIVE

The failure of Operation Market-Garden gave the Nazis a welcome breathing space. Hitler gathered his remaining forces for one final offensive. He caught the Allies unprepared in the Ardennes Offensive – the Battle of the Bulge.

On 16 December, 1944 the Americans received their biggest shock of the war since Pearl Harbor when their positions in eastern Belgium and Luxembourg unexpectedly came under savage enemy attack. Under cover of fog, a quarter of a million Germans, supported by a thousand tanks, had advanced unnoticed through the supposedly impenetrable forests of the Eifel Mountains. Parachute landings behind the lines by Otto Skorzeny's highly trained team of soldiers, disguised as Americans, caused further confusion. Rundstedt, once again placed in charge of a major operation, cautioned Hitler not to advance too far, but the Führer's objective was Antwerp. Initially the Germans created a major salient, a bulge into the Allied front which

Above left: *Soldiers of the Wehrmacht advance into the Bulge, 17 December 1944.* Centre left: *The signal to move forward. The Ardennes Offensive was Hitler's last. Once the weather cleared Allied bombers established their air superiority quickly, and the Germans were forced to retreat into the Reich.* Centre right: *Remains of the victims of the Malmédy Massacre are numbered before the burial. Note the doctor's helmet between the two bodies.* Above right: *Many German soldiers were spirited behind American lines dressed as GIs, after having learned American slang in special camps for months. Most of them were eventually captured. Not to know who the centre fielder of the New York Yankees was, or Popeye's girlfriend's name, meant immediate death. Here one German, dressed as an American, is tied to a post prior to his death before a firing squad.* Below: *German tank passes captured American POWs the day after the surprise attack of the Ardennes Offensive.*

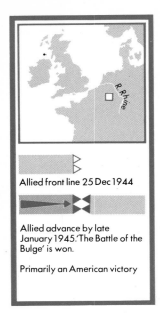

Allied front line 25 Dec 1944

Allied advance by late January 1945. The 'Battle of the Bulge' is won.

Primarily an American victory

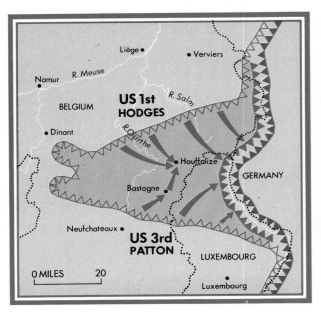

Above right: *General George S. Patton, Jr, who refused to give up Bastogne.* Right: *Bastogne.*

Above: *German prisoners carry one of their wounded after their capture near Wallerode, Belgium, during the Allied counter-offensive in early January 1945.* Above right: *Supplies are dropped to the beleaguered fortress of Bastogne.* Below: *SS General Sepp Dietrich, whose army had the best chance of reaching Antwerp, his objective in the Ardennes Offensive.*

separated the American First Army (commanded by General Hodges) from the Third, under Patton, who refused to abandon Bastogne. At first the Germans were lucky. Heavy fog in England, spreading to the Continent, deprived the Allies of air cover for almost a week. The Luftwaffe was far too weakened to provide support. The Sixth Panzer Army under SS General Sepp Dietrich pressed toward Liège, and the Fifth, under General Hasso von Manteuffel, reached Houffalize and Bastogne. But by the 19th Dietrich was stopped. Hitler would never get his troops to Antwerp. Nevertheless, the German breakthrough had stunned the Allies and tested Eisenhower. It was the first time in World War Two that he had suffered setbacks. He sent Omar Bradley's Twelfth Army Group to attack the south flank of the bulge, and placed his US First and Ninth Armies under Montgomery's command north of the salient. But Patton did not budge from Bastogne. The 101st Airborne Division bolstered the 'battling bastards

of Bastogne' and when Brigadier-General Anthony McAuliffe was ordered to surrender by the Germans, he sent back a one-word reply: 'Nuts!' By Christmas the Allies were staging their counter-thrust.

The weather had cleared. Allied planes were now bombarding the Germans, who, unable to take Bastogne, had bypassed the town at considerable cost to themselves. Manteuffel's spearhead was cut off. By the second week in January Patton had relieved Bastogne and Model and Rundstedt had decided to disengage. The original front line was restored at the end of January. Hitler's last gambler's throw was over. His reserves were spent. A Russian offensive began on 12 January, and Hitler had to withdraw forces in the West to bolster his sagging defences in the East. The Allies had suffered over 75,000 casualties, but the Germans had lost 120,000 men, and, even more costly, 500 tanks and over 1,500 planes. They had fought with their usual daring and courage; that was all they had left.

THE END OF THE DICTATORS

After the fall of Warsaw and the failure to break through in the Ardennes, the Third Reich gathered its forces for a defence of the Fatherland. As British, American and Russian armies raced towards Berlin, the final tragedy in Italy was taking place. Mussolini tried to escape to Switzerland but was caught and executed. Hitler hoped to avoid the fate of Il Duce. As Russian armies reduced Berlin to rubble and pressed toward the Reichschancellery, Hitler prepared his suicide. The 'thousand-year Reich' of Adolf Hitler was consumed in flames.

Hitler's morale was not shaken by the disasters of 1944. Drugged and half-mad, he refused to withdraw 30 divisions from Courland (Latvia), still convinced that his new secret weapon would bring the victory which everyone else now considered impossible. His scientists were working on atomic weapons. Although his new jet fighters, the Me-262 and Me-163, were operational, there were too few of them to make a difference. V-2 rockets were sent over England. But it was all too little, too late. Superior numbers, in both men and materials, were overwhelming the Third Reich. The Luftwaffe scarcely existed. His 'men' were composed of teenage boys and men in their sixties who were called upon to help the battle-weary veterans of dozens of campaigns.

At the end of January 1945, the Big Three – Roosevelt, Churchill and Stalin – met for the last time at Yalta, in the Crimea, to decide the fate of Germany and Japan after the war. The Americans were to occupy Japan, and the Russians would take over Manchuria and Korea down to the 38th Parallel – arrangements which were made more clear at the postwar Potsdam Conference in July 1945. Russia was to regain Port Arthur and southern Sakhalin, seized from her by Japan in 1905; and she was also to have the Japanese Kurile Islands. In return, Stalin promised to enter the war in the Far East two to three months after Germany's capitulation. Germany herself was to be partitioned into three (later four) parts, with each major Allied power occupying a portion. Berlin was to be administered by the same four nations (France being included at Churchill's insistence). The same fate was arranged for Austria. More importantly, it was agreed that the dividing line between Anglo-American and Russian troops was to be the River Elbe. Large parts of eastern Germany were to be given to Poland, while Russia would annex the territory taken from Poland in 1939 as well as Estonia, Latvia and Lithuania, seized in

Top right: Generals Bradley, Eisenhower and Patton survey the ruins of Bastogne after the collapse of the Ardennes Offensive. Centre right: *Over the Rhine at Oberwesel, 26 March 1945.* Bottom right: *Nazi atrocities in the last stages of the war were unspeakable. Latvian Jewish women are forced to strip prior to their mass execution as the Germans withdrew from the Baltic States.* Opposite: *US troops march through the ruins of Saarbrucken, 20 March 1945.*

1940. Königsberg, the capital of East Prussia, was to be directly annexed by the Soviet Union. Stalin felt well satisfied. Roosevelt's generosity can be explained by three factors: the fatal illness which was to end his life on 12 April; his over-confidence in his ability to 'handle Uncle Joe'; and his desire to give assistance to the American forces in the Far East, whose greatest sacrifices still lay ahead.

If the Russians were to gain the most from the war, they sacrificed the most as well. With almost twenty million of their countrymen already dead, they launched their final great offensive on 12 January. Five days later they finally took Warsaw. As Koniev swept through southern Poland, Zhukov pushed through the centre, and Rokossovsky took the northern route, devastating East Prussia in his wake. By early February the Oder had been crossed. The Russians were within 40 miles of Berlin. By this time the Ardennes campaign was over. The Anglo-Americans wiped out Dresden, a target of no military importance whatever, on 13–14 February, killing 135,000 civilians and refugees huddled in the beautiful medieval city. Twice as many people died in Dresden as in Hiroshima. But the Anglo-Americans hit every city with a population of 100,000 or more, sparing only Wiesbaden and Heidelberg, which were destined to be headquarters towns for the US occupation forces after the war. By early March Anglo-American forces reached the Rhine, and the Remagen Bridge, amazingly intact after the heavy bombardment Germany experienced, was crossed. By 13 March the whole of the west bank of the Rhine was in Allied hands. The Germans continued to fight valiantly for the Fatherland, and the losses were staggering. On 28 March the Russians began their saturation bombing of Berlin. The Ruhr underwent a double envelopment, caught between the US First and Ninth Armies. Model and his 400,000 men were trapped, and on 21 April he shot himself. On 12 April, the day Roosevelt died, the Americans crossed the Elbe, only 60 miles from Berlin. On the following day the Russians took Vienna.

Stalin, counting on Roosevelt's good will, had been in no great hurry to take Berlin, which was, in any case, doomed. But if the new American President, Harry S. Truman, felt disinclined to honour the Yalta agreements (which he was only to learn about after taking office), everything might be jeopardized. So the race for Berlin was

on. Stalin threw two and a half million men, over 6,000 tanks and 7,500 aircraft against Berlin on 16 April. Six days later, with Patton's forces halted after entering Czechoslovakia, Russian troops marched into the besieged capital. In Italy, meanwhile, the front had broken as well, and Allied soldiers streamed into the Po Valley. Mussolini tried to escape to Switzerland, but was caught when recognized. He and his mistress, Clara Petacci, were shot on 28 April. The following day their bodies were hung upside down on meat hooks and mutilated by crowds in Milan.

Hitler, trapped for weeks in the subterranean bunker under his Chancellery, now knew the end was at hand. Imagining that Roosevelt's death was another miracle for Berlin (he compared it to the Tsarina Elizabeth's death in 1762 which saved his hero, Frederick the Great, and Berlin from the Russian forces which surrounded them in the Seven Years War), he was shocked into reality at last. On the night of 28–29 April, he married his mistress, Eva Braun, in a macabre ceremony in the bunker. He wrote out his political testament – a final diatribe against the Jews whom he had done his best to annihilate – and his will. He appointed Admiral Karl Doenitz as his successor. On 30 April he said farewell to his staff, poisoned his Alsatian dog, Blondi, and his new wife, and then shot himself. Their bodies were cremated outside the bunker. Russian troops were only two streets away; Berlin was ablaze around the burial team. Goebbels poisoned himself, his wife and children. Admiral Doenitz wasted no time in capitulating. The unconditional surrender was signed in Rheims on 7 May. The war in Europe was over.

Right: *Mussolini and his mistress, Clara Petacci, are hung by their heels in a square in Milan after they were killed trying to escape to Switzerland.* Centre right: *General Patton and Marshal Zhukov review the victory parade in occupied Berlin celebrating the Allied triumph over Japan; September 1945.*

Above: *Admiral Doenitz is escorted into captivity. He was named the Second Führer of the Third Reich after Hitler committed suicide in the Berlin bunker.*

Top left: *Roosevelt, Churchill and Stalin dine during the Yalta Conference, which partitioned Germany and Europe. Stalin promised Roosevelt that Russia would enter the Far Eastern war two or three months after the Nazi capitulation. He kept his word, three months to the day after V-E Day. The Soviet Union annexed huge territories in Europe and Asia and gained effective control over Eastern Europe thanks to the decisions made at this meeting.* Above centre: *German prisoners march through the burning city of Magdeburg in the final days of the Third Reich.* Above right: *Nazi POWs are marched down the autobahn near Giessen as vehicles of the 6th Armored Division, Third Army, roll past them.* Below: *Wrecked vehicles lie among the rubble-littered grounds of the Reichstag building in Berlin.*

RETURN TO THE PHILIPPINES

General Douglas MacArthur promised to return to the Philippines to avenge Bataan and Corregidor. The fight to free them from Japanese rule was one of the most bitterly fought contests in the war.

By mid-1944 most of New Guinea was in Allied hands. The American Navy was pushing steadily toward Japan. Blocking the way were the Marianas and the Philippines. The island of Saipan in the Marianas was only 1,350 miles from Tokyo. It was considered an impregnable fortress even by the Americans, and the Japanese regarded it almost as home territory. If America breached the Marianas barrier, there was virtually no hope for Japan. Realizing that the Japanese would fight harder as the Allies approached, Admiral Nimitz amassed a huge fleet under the leadership of Admiral Kelly Turner – more than 500 ships and over 125,000 men. General Yoshitsugu Saito on Saipan had only 22,000. The Japanese navy under the overall command of Admiral Soemu Toyoda, although outnumbered by almost three to one in ships and by two to one in planes, came out to meet the American fleet. Toyoda was determined to stop the Americans before they reached the Philippines and, by doing so, prevent the loss of Saipan. On 19 June his planes struck the US Navy without warning. The Japanese scored only one hit and lost 45 of their 69 planes in the first wave of what came to be known as the Great Marianas Turkey Shoot. Two Japanese carriers, *Shokaku* and *Tahio*, were hit by submarines and sunk. In the second wave, Japan lost 98 out of 130 planes. The third wave missed its targets entirely, and in the fourth, only nine of the 82 planes returned. Against a total of 346 Japanese planes shot down, the Americans lost only 30. Japanese pilots were exceptionally brave and daring, but they were poorly trained. The Battle of the Philippine Sea was an unmitigated disaster for Japan. On 19—20 June Vice-Admiral Isaburo Ozawa's main fleet was pursued and caught. Ozawa lost over 400 of the 435 planes he sent out, along with the carrier *Hiyo*. Another carrier, the *Zuikaku*, was badly damaged and many smaller vessels were also sunk. The Japanese started out with five carriers and were left with only one that was operational after the battle, while the Americans had all seven intact, with a loss of only 130 planes. With pressure eased, despite fierce

resistance the Americans secured Saipan only a fortnight later. The fate of Guam, the other vital fortress in the Marianas, was sealed as well.

The great disaster in the Philippine Sea was concealed from even high officials in Tokyo, but the loss of Saipan could not be covered up. The Japanese people became aware for the first time in the war that defeat was not only possible but likely. Hideki Tojo, the wartime Premier who ordered the attack on Pearl Harbor, was forced to resign in mid-July, on the day that the loss of Saipan was officially announced. The army chose one of their number to succeed him, but the loss of face was apparent for all to see. Japan had to make a successful stand soon or face invasion and national disaster.

The loss of Saipan was a shattering blow to Japanese morale. When Guam fell on 10 August, 12,000 defenders were captured. This was very unusual, as the Bushido code demanded death before dishonour, and there could be nothing more dishonourable than surrender. By September it had been decided that Formosa was too strongly defended to be taken, and that both Nimitz and MacArthur would participate in the clearing of the Philippines. Admiral William ('Bull') Halsey hammered Japanese airfields on the Philippine coast from his aircraft carriers, and met little opposition. The whole programme was speeded up; and at the Quebec Conference in September Churchill and Roosevelt decided to attack Leyte in the Philippines on 20 October.

In the preliminaries to the invasion of Leyte, Formosa was bombed and the Japanese lost another 500 planes trying to protect airfields there and in coastal China. Then MacArthur took the bold stroke of advancing ahead of his air cover to land his forces on Leyte on 20 October, albeit with the protection of a massive fleet assembled by Nimitz – over 700 ships, including seventeen carriers. His plan was to attract the remainder of the Japanese Navy in order to deliver it a fatal blow. Within two days there were 130,000 Americans on Leyte.

Ozawa, following the course set by Yamamoto at Pearl Harbor and Midway, still hoped to deliver a *coup de grace* to the US Navy. Though now deprived of enough planes to attack American ships effectively, he relied on the firepower of his capital ships to save his fleet and homeland. Most formidable of all was the *Yamato* displacing 64,000 tons, the largest battleship in the world, with 18-inch guns. He still had four carriers, far too few for victory. Ozawa had not learned the great lesson of the Pacific naval war: that without carriers and sufficient planes, any battle fleet, however powerful, is helpless against air attack.

Top left: Hundreds of boats race through the water towards their landing in Leyte in October 1944. Top right: A kamikaze *attack on the USS* White Plains *during the landings on the Philippines, 25 October 1944. A 20-mm anti-aircraft gun is firing at the left while the ship appears to be making a sharp turn to avoid the crash dive of the Zero. Left: General Douglas MacArthur, surrounded by US and Philippine officials, wades ashore at Leyte.*

Left: *Rear-Admiral Raymond Spruance, under whose command US naval forces crossed the Pacific to decimate the Japanese fleet in the Battle of the Philippine Sea, the last great carrier battle. Above centre: Japanese General Tomoyuki Yamashita, the 'Tiger of Malaya', who conducted a brilliant if brutal rear-guard action in Luzon during the closing stages of the Philippine campaign, tying up thousands of American troops. Above: Vice-Admiral Shoji Nishimura, commanding officer of the second battleship division which fought at Leyte Gulf.*

Far left: *Marines advance on Saipan. The marine in the centre has just been hit by a sniper's bullet.* Centre left: *Rear-Admiral Jesse Oldendorf.* Above left: *A salvo from the Japanese super-battleship* Yamato *lands near the USS* Hoel *during the battle off Samar, 25 October 1944.* Above right: *The Battle of Leyte Gulf destroyed the remainder of the Japanese fleet.*

This was seen again in the Battle of Leyte Gulf.

The Japanese approached from two directions: Ozawa from Japan; Vice-Admiral Takeo Kurita from Borneo. Ozawa hoped to lure Halsey's force to the north – a plan which worked, leaving MacArthur's troops on Leyte. While Halsey pursued Ozawa, Kurita, despite the sinking of his flagship by US submarines on 23 October, sent his forces in to attack what he thought was the unprotected squadron under Admiral Thomas Kincaid. He scored some victories, including the destroyer *Johnston*, but US planes launched from the carriers badly damaged his fleet. On 25 October the first desperate *kamikaze* (Divine Wind) raids were launched – one-way journeys by fanatical Japanese pilots who sent their planes crashing directly on American ships. On the same day Halsey found Ozawa and sank all four of his carriers, then returned to find the battle in the south over. He had left MacArthur and Kincaid, as well as Rear-Admiral Clifton Sprague, in charge of Kincaid's escort carriers, to the hands of fate. But it was not fate which sealed the doom of the Japanese Navy. It was American air power, courage and daring under fire, and the unwillingness of Japanese admirals to risk their beloved ships which cost them the last great naval battle of the war. The Japanese Fleet virtually ceased to exist after the Battle of Leyte Gulf.

The suicidal *kamikaze* attacks against American ships were stepped up as US forces dug in on Leyte. The raids were as terrifying as they were mad, and many convoys were badly damaged. But they were of no avail. By January 1945 the Japanese had used up practically every plane they had in the area, and General Yamashita's forces on Luzon, the main island of the Philippines, were exposed to constant air attack. On 4 January US troops returned to Luzon. The Japanese made a stand in Manila which was defended with typical fanaticism. The beautiful Intramuros section of the city was obliterated before the capital was secured in early March. The Americans were obliged to fight it out in the jungles of the Philippines, island by island. Lt.-General Robert Eichelberger, Commander of the US Eighth Army, made almost daily

amphibious landings forcing Yamashita into a pocket in northern Luzon, where he continued to resist until the end of the war.

MacArthur had fulfilled his promise to return. The taking of the Philippines was his last campaign. For the remainder of the war he was preparing for the projected invasion of Japan (preceded by a naval assault) which he estimated would involve five million men and cost at least a million American lives. But by sacrificing what remained of her fleet and air force in Leyte Gulf, Japan had played her final card. She had nothing left except her courage and stubborn will to resist to the last man.

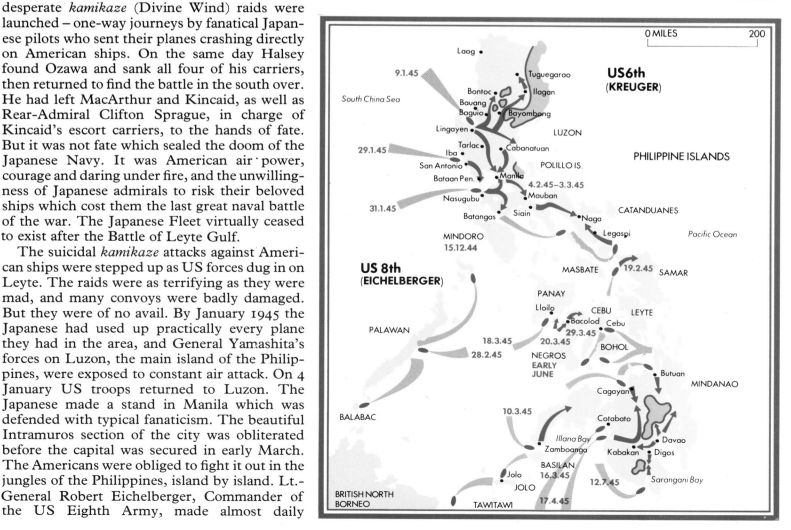

BURMA & THE CBI

The British Empire had suffered irreparable reverses in Malaya and Burma in 1942. By 1945 General Slim avenged the honour of the British Army in the Burma campaign.

Above: *'Vinegar Joe' Stilwell eats with the troops on Christmas morning 1943. The breakfast amounted to just another day's C rations.* Below: *Major General Claire Chennault (left), Commander of the 14th Air Force in China, greets Major General Albert Wedemeyer upon his arrival when he replaced Stilwell as Commander of American Forces in China. Wedemeyer found it easier to get along with Chiang Kai-shek.*

When Burma and South-East Asia fell to Japan in 1942, the Nationalist Chinese under Generalissimo Chiang Kai-shek were cut off. Their road links through Burma to India were controlled by Japan, so an airlift was mounted in the CBI (China–Burma–India) Theatre of Operations to fly supplies to Chungking, the provisional Chinese capital, over the 'Hump' of the Himalayas from India. Chiang's regime was thoroughly corrupt. The hundreds of millions of dollars-worth of aid poured annually into Chungking from Washington lined the pockets of high-ranking generals; and as a result of nepotism and direct bribery some of the money found its way down the hierarchy. Even more important, however, was the fact that Chiang and his generals would not fight the Japanese. General Joseph ('Vinegar Joe') Stilwell was sent out by Roosevelt to see what he could do to remedy the situation, but his efforts were frustrated. Eventually he alienated both Roosevelt and Chiang and was recalled. Despite the valiant efforts of Major General Claire Chennault, whose Flying Tigers helped Chiang before Pearl Harbor and afterwards as part of the 14th Air Force, Chinese pilots were more interested in drawing pay and doing a little business on the side than in fighting. Chiang himself claimed that the main enemy was Communism and Mao Tse-tung. America, however, was giving Chiang money and pilots to fight Japan and Chennault's 14th Air Force was doing just that, establishing airfields in eastern China, then harassing and bombing Japanese port and other installations on the south China coast and in Indo-China. Japan retaliated by launching a counter-offensive to close the gap between her occupied territories (administered by their puppet Chinese dictator, Wang Ching-wei) and the Indo-Chinese border. This gap was closed during the Japanese offensive of 1944 as troops pushed hundreds of miles inland along a broad front in the direction of Chungking.

But Chiang still refused to fight with any degree of determination. Inflation was rife in Nationalist China; and bribery was necessary to keep some semblance of order within the army. Heavy fighting might evoke a general rising or, at worse, a total collapse. The US was saddled with a lame duck, but it was a necessary evil. For if the Nationalists collapsed, millions of Japanese soldiers would be available for duty in the Pacific, and the vast natural resources of China would be open to Japanese exploitation. Roosevelt saw that America's main duty was to keep China in the war.

Above: *Curtiss P-40s of the Flying Tigers attack Japanese air fields in south China.*

Above: *Japanese infantry move forward toward Kohima, where the fiercest fighting of the entire Burma campaign took place.*

Above: *Generalissimo Chiang Kai-shek, leader of Nationalist China, preferred to husband his resources for the fight against the Communists rather than 'to waste' them against the Japanese. The Allies were fighting Japan in World War II. Above right: Flying Tigers over the 'Hump' of the Himalayas brought billions of dollars worth of equipment into Chungking.*

thereby materially aiding Chiang, and at the same time restore their lost colony to the Empire. This was Britain's aim in 1943, after the creation of the 'Free India' government of Subhas Chandra Bose and his Indian National Army by the Japanese in Singapore. While Japan was revitalizing or creating nationalist movements in former British and Dutch colonies, the return of these areas to their respective empires after the war was over would be difficult if not impossible. That was why it was vital for Britain to make a firm stand somewhere in South-East Asia. For although the region was not strategically essential for the final defeat of Japan, it could only be regained if the subject peoples were to see Europeans actually engaging and defeating the Japanese on the ground.

Lord Louis Mountbatten was appointed Commander-in-Chief South-East Asia in 1943. He formed a new army, composed of recruits whose chief interests were political, and elements of the old Indian Army, who looked upon the newcomers with disdain. Morale was low; they called themselves 'the forgotten army'. In the field defending the north-east frontier of India were men plagued by malaria, dysentery, typhus and all the other wretched torments of jungle warfare. Mountbatten decided to pursue a forward policy with the aim of rebuilding morale and re-establishing a land communication link with Nationalist China. Supplies sent over the

Above: *British troops move forward on the road to Mandalay during the campaign to drive the Japanese out of Burma.* Left: *British and Indian troops drive forward on the Kohima-Imphal road. Gurkhas and men of the West Yorkshire Regiment advance under cover of their tanks.* Right: *Lieutenant-General William Slim, commander of the 14th Army which cleared Burma of Japanese forces in 1944–45.*

Chiang, however, was the wiser of the two. He knew, with General George C. Marshall of the Joint Chiefs of Staff, that Japan could not be conquered through China. Allied strategy was to move as quickly as possible against Japan herself. Thus, Chiang knew that he did not need to fight – only continue to exist. He recognized that an Allied victory was inevitable. His reconquest of China was not. So he waited for the end of the war in order to reassert his authority over the whole of China before the Communists did.

The British had a dual purpose in helping Chiang. Co-operation with the US was desirable, of course, but by clearing Burma the British could reopen the Burma Road to Kunming,

Left: *A British soldier leads a Japanese prisoner past a burning Burmese hut.* Above: *Fighting near a pagoda in Mandalay. The drive through Burma was one of the most thankless tasks the British Army undertook in a campaign which was almost forgotten by the public.*

'Hump' were doubled. Chennault began setting up his airfields in eastern China. Meanwhile an Allied drive would aim for Myitkyina and its airstrips. Stilwell's army in China was to come down the Chindwin River while Chindits (77th Indian Infantry Brigade) under Orde Wingate were dropped behind Japanese lines to hinder communications. In Arakan the XV Corps was to retake Akyab.

The Arakan offensive was initially a failure. The Japanese outflanked and surrounded the British, who, in these circumstances, usually withdrew. This time, having control of the air, they stood firm. This change of tactics surprised the Japanese, who began to surrender for the first time, indicating a change in their morale as well. On 15 March, 1944 the Japanese took the offensive in an attempt to invade India and overrun the airbases from which flights were being made over the 'Hump'. By June Field Marshal William Slim had built up his forces at Kohima and Imphal. By July the siege of Imphal had been lifted and the outnumbered Japanese began their retreat. Kohima, Imphal and the retreat which followed it were unmitigated disasters for Japan. Of an army of 85,000 the Japanese lost 53,000 men and most of their tanks. Disorganization in their command, combined with British air superiority, created the worst defeat for Japanese armies in the war. Although they fought doggedly, they were now in full retreat as the Allies re-entered Burma. The news of the defeat of 4 July reached Tokyo at the same time as the news of the fall of Paris. The Japanese High Command began to realize that all was lost. Men were needed to defend the home islands. Burma was to get no further support. Americans and Chinese attacked Burma from the north, while the British pursued their opponents into north-west Burma. Myitkyina was taken on 4 August by Stilwell,

who was recalled in October because of pressures on Washington exerted by Chiang Kai-shek.

By February 1945 the Allied offensive had reached Meiktila, where the last major battle occurred. The Japanese fought with insane fury to block the way to this vital communications centre, but to no avail. Mandalay fell on 20 March, and the road to Rangoon was open. The race to reach Rangoon before the coming of the monsoon was also won, the British liberating the Burmese capital on 3 May. The rest of the campaign amounted to a clean-up operation.

Burma was the only campaign in the Far Eastern war in which the British distinguished themselves. The Americans were anxious to keep them out of the main action in the Pacific; and in any event, Britain had quite enough to keep her busy, first in the Desert, then in Italy and France. Roosevelt wanted to prevent a revival of Western imperialism in the Far East, feeling that the future lay with the nationalist forces in South and South-East Asia, many of whom were encouraged and promoted by the Japanese. The argument has been put forward that the war in Burma need not have been fought at all. It did not end the war one day sooner. Heat, disease and danger made the jungle a hell for British and Japanese soldiers alike. But face had been saved for the British Empire, not only in Eastern eyes, but in the eyes of the British themselves. They were to relinquish their Indian Empire in 1947, while an independent Burma left the Commonwealth in 1948. So the Burma campaign, though courageous, was, in retrospect, somewhat pointless, and understandably lowest on the priority list, both in terms of equipment and men. Nevertheless, the men who fought there behaved heroically, none more so than the modest victor, William Slim. His quiet bravery was an inspiration to those who served under him.

THE FINAL ASSAULT

The closer the Allies got to the home islands of Japan, the harder the Japanese fought. The intensity of the Japanese defence of Iwo Jima and Okinawa convinced the Americans that the use of a secret weapon was the only way to shorten the war. This weapon inaugurated a new age and ended the war in the Pacific: the atomic bomb.

The closer the Americans got to Japan, the harder the Japanese fought. One of the most bitter struggles in the entire war came at Iwo Jima, a tiny island important only for its two airfields. Halfway between Saipan and Japan, it could be used by fighter planes to escort the B-29s, which had begun bombing raids of Japan in November 1944. The Japanese dug in on Iwo Jima, hiding in caves and foxholes all over the island. Admiral Nimitz entrusted the assault to Admiral Raymond Spruance, and three Marine divisions hit the beaches on 19 February, 1945. They had to take the island and its prominent feature, Mount Surabachi, literally yard by yard. Five weeks were needed to conquer the island in some of the most ferocious fighting in the war. The Americans lost 26,000 men, about 30 per cent of their strike force. In the campaign and in the two-month-long clean-up operation which followed, some 25,000 Japanese were killed. Only about a thousand prisoners were taken.

Next on the list was Okinawa, a long island in the Ryukyus only 340 miles from Japan. The Americans landed there on 1 April, meeting no initial opposition. The airfields were taken and all seemed to be going well until 6 April. Then the Japanese sent in the gem of her navy, the battleship *Yamato*. It was a *kamikaze* mission. With only enough fuel for a one-way trip, her assignment was to destroy as much as possible until she was sunk. On 7 April, after intense aerial attack, she went down with all hands – almost 2,500 men. This suicidal mission convinced the Americans that Japan would have to be reduced to ashes and taken inch by inch, like Iwo Jima, before she would capitulate. The Americans lost only fifteen planes, while in addition to the *Yamato* they sank a light cruiser and eight destroyers. Japan now only had one battleship left. Yet she still hurled over 3,000 *kamikaze* pilots against the 170,000 Americans who had now landed on Okinawa. The Japanese army, 110,000 strong, was dug in across the centre of the island. Lt.-General Mitsuru Ushijima ordered his men to fight until death. They fought fatalistically, fanatically, resolutely. The American casualty rate in the three-month battle was extraordinarily high – over 49,000, including

Left: D-Day, H-Hour at Iwo Jima as the US landing party approached the beach. Mount Surabachi, where the Marines finally raised the Stars and Stripes in triumph, is in the background. Below: Landing craft approach Iwo Jima. Some of the most savage fighting of the war took place on this remote and bleak island, but its seizure was vital, for its airstrip could be used against Japan itself. Right: Fourth Marine Division drop to the deck as they hit the beach of Iwo Jima. Enemy fire sprayed them as they landed in an LSM (in the background).

Above: *The biggest battleship built in World War II, the* Yamato, *is fitted out at Kure in 1941, with the carrier* Hosho *in the background. The* Yamato *carried out its own* kamikaze *mission at Okinawa in a final, desperate but futile gamble to stop the Allied thrust toward Japan.* Below: *The charred and mangled body of a Japanese soldier, who attempted a commando raid on Yontan air field in Okinawa, lies pinned under the wing of one of the attacking planes.*

Above left: *A* kamikaze *attack on the USS* Missouri *off Okinawa. The Japanese surrender was signed on board the* Missouri *a few months later.* Top centre: *US Marine Corps Corsair fires rockets at the Japanese trapped in the caves of the rugged terrain on Okinawa.* Lower centre: *Marine patrols of the Sixth Division hunt for Japanese snipers in the city of Naha on Okinawa.* Above right: *Troops of the 96th Division, the first American soldiers to land on Okinawa, climb a sea wall.*

some 12,000 killed – the most costly US campaign of the war. The Japanese lost virtually their entire defence force. On 22 June, the day after the surrender, Ushijima and his Chief of Staff committed *hara-kiri* in full dress uniform, maintaining the code of Bushido to the bitter end.

With the war in Europe over, it was clear that Japan was finished. But if it took almost 50,000 American casualties to take Okinawa, how many would be required to conquer Japan? The skies over the home islands were filled with bombers and their deadly cargo, battering Japanese cities by day and by night. Yet there was still no surrender. When the Potsdam Conference was held in July, Churchill and Truman were aware that an atomic bomb had been successfully exploded at a testing site in New Mexico. They informed Stalin that America had a new and more powerful weapon, but his face remained impassive. In fact, Russian agents in the US had already informed the Soviet government of the existence of the bomb. The Allies saw no reason not to use it if it would hasten the end of the war. It was also revealed at Potsdam, however, that the Japanese had made tentative approaches to the Swedish government to work out surrender terms. Yet the resistance on Iwo Jima and Okinawa convinced Truman that Japanese talks meant little; he recalled that they had still been talking peace on Pearl Harbor day. On 26 July the Big Three announced the terms they would accept from Japan – unconditional surrender, a renunciation of all colonies, and military occupation. On 30 July the Prime Minister, Admiral Kantaro Suzuki, gave his reply. He would not only refuse to comment; he treated the offer with contempt. At this point Truman decided to use

the bomb. In the back of his mind, of course, was the Soviet deadline for entering the Far East conflict – 8 August. He wanted to give the Russians no excuse to intervene in the war which was already virtually won. At Yalta Roosevelt felt he needed Soviet help. At Potsdam Truman knew that he did not.

Hiroshima was the target of the first atomic bomb to be dropped in war. Four B-29s appeared on the morning of 6 August, 1945. One superfortress, the *Enola Gay*, under the command of Colonel Paul Tibbets, released a single bomb attached to parachutes. It descended for five miles and then burst over its target. Of at least 125,000 casualties, the majority were killed outright. They were the lucky ones. Over a generation later there are still people suffering from radiation, many bearing hideous scars as reminders of that terrible morning. The bomb was small by modern standards, only equivalent to 10,000 tons of TNT. Yet everything went up in flames. The heat on the ground was scorching. There was virtually nothing left of Hiroshima. Truman sent another ultimatum to the Japanese government, which was already considering surrender. It was ignored.

On 8 August, three months to the day after the victory in Europe, the Soviet Union invaded Manchuria. The following day another atomic bomb was dropped on Nagasaki. On 14 August Japan accepted the Potsdam Declaration. On 2 September, aboard the *Missouri*, General MacArthur accepted Japan's formal unconditional surrender. Soviet troops were still pouring into Manchuria and Korea. Even as the greatest conflict in the history of the world ended, the spirit of impending Cold War hovered over the scene.

Above: *The Japanese fought to the last man on Okinawa. The few survivors were badly mutilated.* Left and right: *The first atomic bomb in warfare: Hiroshima, 6 August 1945.*

War Crimes Tribunals were set up in Germany, Japan and other countries to try the so-called war criminals. At Nuremberg Goering, Ribbentrop, Himmler and nine others were sentenced to death and executed; others, like Speer and Hess, got long prison terms. In Tokyo Tojo and six colleagues were hanged. Many thousands more found their way to prison in the decades following World War Two. Some are facing trial even now, over 30 years afterwards. The morality of these trials has often been called into question. Clearly those responsible for millions of deaths of innocent civilians in concentration camps carry a heavy burden of guilt. But what of those who administered slave labour camps? What about soldiers who executed civilians or partisans in the field? And what of those who did the dirty work but claimed they only were carrying out orders issued from above, the only alternative being their own imprisonment or death? There is no easy answer to this question, just as there is no easy answer to the reasons for bombing Dresden, making fire-raids on Hamburg, or creating rubble out of practically every large German and Japanese city. The crimes committed by Russia in the war were countless. Suffice it to say that thanks to Stalin, millions of civilians were killed, tortured, raped, imprisoned or worked to death in forced labour gangs. The Americans dropped two atomic bombs on essentially civilian targets in order to hasten the end of the war. Are any of these actions right according to the standards set by our own ideals and religious beliefs?

The only conclusion must be that war in itself is an unspeakable crime against humanity. Twentieth-century warfare involves whole populations, not merely soldiers on the battlefield. Human nature, subject to error at the best of times, tends to deviate even more under pressure.

The Allies made remarkable mistakes before, during, and after the war. Thanks to Britain and France, Hitler gained great successes before the war ever began. American isolationists learned the wrong lessons from World War One, opposing US participation until woken from their slumbers by Pearl Harbor – an attack which extended the war in Asia and unduly prolonged the war in Europe. The Russians helped Hitler for two years before he invaded their soil. Finally, by insisting on terms of unconditional surrender, the Western Allies not only prolonged the war in Europe and Asia for at least a year, but opened Eastern Europe to the tyranny of Stalin which did not end with his death. The Berlin Wall and the bloody events of Czechoslovakia and Hungary were the work of his successors. What would have been the fate of the leaders of the West if Hitler had won the war?

It is no good trying to set an example by emulating those whom we vilify. After the war we tried and convicted those whose actions we detested. Our readiness to continue to do so after all these years is a continuation of a policy that was open to serious objection even in the wake of wartime propaganda. It is impossible to separate war crime from war. If the Nuremberg and Tokyo War Crimes Trials were taken to their illogical conclusion, all those who actively participated in killing should be tried, whether they fought on the Axis or the Allied side. By singling out those who acted with particular brutality or efficiency, we give ourselves no credit. Nations who fought the war were not punished by the trials of their leaders and eventually many of their underlings. They had been punished enough. Germany and Japan were utterly destroyed. They lost millions of people, many of them civilians. America lost almost 300,000; Britain, 450,000; France, about 500,000; Russia at least 20 million. The final total of casualties on all sides, both civilian and military, must have been at least 50 million. Did the deaths of a few more after the war mitigate this human suffering one iota?

Recreating the emotions of a war long since over makes no sense. One must think in a more positive way. In order to prevent another tragedy like World War Two, its real lessons should be learned. Military weakness, not military strength, invites war. To make savings on armaments spending by governments in favour of more immediately constructive expenditure is laudable in the short term, but ultimately fatal. Neutrality and disarmament did not save Britain, America, Holland, Norway, Denmark and the others from the evils of war. The nations who began the war all lost. The only real victors were Russia and America, who stayed out as long as they could; yet they too paid for their unpreparedness. There have always been wars in history. As long as there is human error, there always will be. When the drums begin to roll again, as inevitably and regrettably they must, those who are best prepared will have the best chance of survival.

Below: *Reichsmarschall Hermann Goering in the dock at Nuremberg. On his left are Rudolf Hess and Joachim von Ribbentrop. Behind sit Karl Doenitz and Erich Raeder. Goering gave an impressive performance in his trial, but he was condemned to death.*

Above: *The ruins of Hiroshima after the atomic attack. Over 80,000 people were killed.* Below: *The deck of the battleship Missouri, 2 September 1945, where Japan unconditionally surrendered to General MacArthur, ending World War II.*

Index

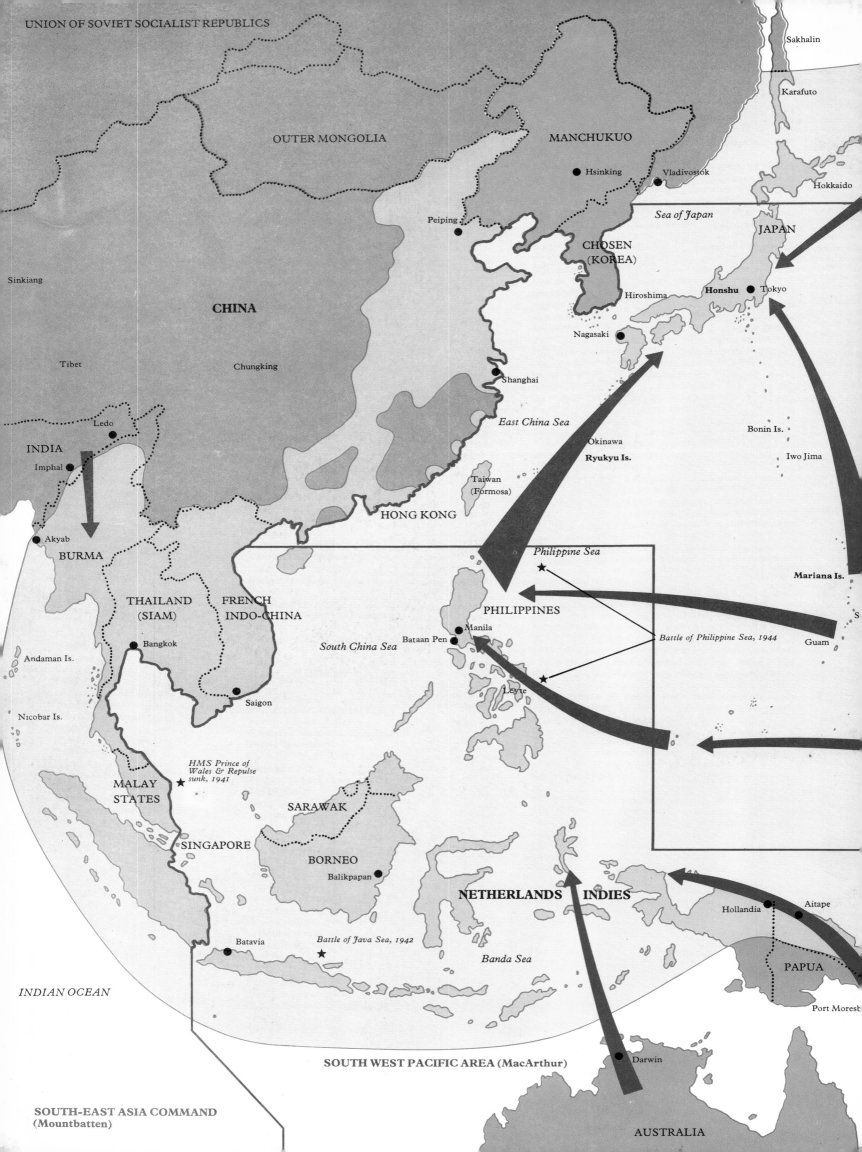

UNION OF SOVIET SOCIALIST REPUBLICS

OUTER MONGOLIA

MANCHUKUO

● Hsinking

Vladivostok ●

Peiping ●

SINKIANG

CHINA

CHOSEN
(KOREA)

Sea of Japan

Sakhalin

Karafuto

Hokkaido

JAPAN

Honshu ● Tokyo

Hiroshima

Nagasaki ●

● Shanghai

East China Sea

Tibet

Chungking

Ledo ●

INDIA

Imphal ●

Akyab ●

BURMA

THAILAND
(SIAM)

FRENCH
INDO-CHINA

Bangkok ●

Andaman Is.

Nicobar Is.

Saigon ●

HONG KONG

Okinawa
RYUKYU Is.

Taiwan
(Formosa)

Bonin Is.

Iwo Jima

Philippine Sea

★

PHILIPPINES

Manila ●
Bataan Pen ●

Mariana Is.

Battle of Philippine Sea, 1944

Guam

South China Sea

★

Leyte

★ HMS Prince of
Wales & Repulse
sunk, 1941

MALAY
STATES

SARAWAK

SINGAPORE

BORNEO

Balikpapan ●

NETHERLANDS   INDIES

Hollandia ● Aitape ●

Battia ●

Battle of Java Sea, 1942

★

Banda Sea

PAPUA

Port Moresb

INDIAN OCEAN

SOUTH WEST PACIFIC AREA (MacArthur)

Darwin ●

SOUTH-EAST ASIA COMMAND
(Mountbatten)

AUSTRALIA